To my mother and to my grandmothers, who have taught me family household secrets and inspired me to create a lovely home. I hope to inspire my daughter Valentina to do the same one day.

French Chic Living

Simple Ways to Make Your Home Beautiful

Florence de Dampierre

Photography by Tim Street-Porter

RIZZOLI
NEW YORK

New York · Paris · London · Milan

CONTENTS

INTRODUCTION

What is more agreeable than one's home?

—CICERO

MY HOUSE IS my sanctuary. I savor every moment I spend there. My French upbringing, with its wonderful, yet practical traditions, has provided me with the foundation for making my home in the United States a pleasure not only for me but also for my family and friends.

Childhood memories of time spent at my grandmother's house and my parent's home in France have inspired my way of living. I marvel at the French rules for the *art de vivre* (art of living), which come from a long tradition. The essence of French style can be summed up in the word *"goût,"* which essentially means "taste." This concept can be traced to the end of the seventeenth century and is forever linked with the dazzling court life at Versailles, where Louis XIV established a culture of luxury, beauty, etiquette, elegance, and quality that still dictates many details of French life—from perfumes to fashion, from food and cuisine to the sophisticated *art de la table* (art of the table).

In France the expressions *bon goût* (good taste), *mauvais goût* (bad taste), and *erreur de goût* (in poor taste) are used all the time. These phrases are applied to everything from one's clothes and hair to one's home. Being told something is in bad taste is the ultimate insult as the French are highly sensitive to aesthetics. *Nouveau riche* is another serious crime. Totally good taste, *bon chic* or *bon genre*, is too

conventional. Instead, infuse your style with personality and flair.

So how should one proceed to achieve a stylish lifestyle? It can be so confusing. This useful guide will provide you with the elements to make your home warm and lovely as well as functional and comfortable. Captivating images of my friends' charming *maison de famille* (family house) in Burgundy illustrate the French ways of making your house a dream—from tidying up to beautifying.

In the pages to come, I present many tips for today's busy lifestyle. From traditional French cleaning solutions to recipes for effortless entertaining, I cover the basics. Learn how to shop for fresh produce at farmers' markets, like the French do. These markets are still the heart and soul of many French towns. Grow your own flavorful herbs, fruits, and vegetables. Make entertaining easier with a well-stocked pantry. You will be at the ready with olives, homemade jams, and vinaigrette. Expertly arrange simple floral bouquets. Pretty pink roses and yellow tulips in a porcelain vase are particularly lovely and will last a long time. Make your home ready to receive unexpected guests. And, always bring a certain *joie de vivre* to your entertaining. A sense of whimsy through decoration will provide joy.

In France vanity is considered more of a virtue than a vice. Rigorous self-maintenance

is our birthright and a mark of pride. French women keep slim not through sweaty spin classes but by following a strict regime that mixes discipline with self-pampering. To keep yourself in shape, follow my grandmother's recipes for health and beauty. Apply home-made preparations to your body and drink healthy *tisanes* (teas).

Indulge, like the French do, without guilt and calorie counting. Learn to take small helpings of each course and watch your alcohol intake. A croissant dunked into coffee for breakfast, a glass of wine at lunch, cakes or cookies at teatime, and escargots at dinner are pleasurable in small quantities. Remember, quality over quantity is the French motto.

Se mettre en valeur, which means "make the most of yourself," is a frequently used French phrase, and intrinsic to the French outlook. A sloppy appearance, either in your person or your home, is considered a serious offense.

By French standards, to let yourself go is one of the worst sins a woman can commit. Do not wear your comfortable, unflattering sweat pants to the market. Remember to stay *soigné* throughout the day. That is the French chic way. And never, ever wear shorts in Paris—as I have tried to explain to my teenage daughter on numerous occasions. It is a sure sign of a tourist. Apply this same philosophy to your home for a beautiful result.

Living *à la Française* is embracing life with its ups and downs, and making the best of it all with elegance. Look and feel your best, make your home tailored to fit your lifestyle, and create a seductive haven. Remember, seduction is the spice of life. In France, everyone seduces everyone all the time. A French chic lifestyle is all about seduction, elegance, and personality.

Voilà. Discover French chic living and let the magic begin.

Chapter One

THE
KITCHEN

I have many fond memories of the time spent in my grandmother's homey country kitchen in Normandy. The space was not fancy but the food that was produced there was delicious and healthy, and it smelled heavenly. All of the ingredients used in her recipes were either grown in the vegetable garden or purchased from local farmers. Her kitchen was the heart of her house for my cousins, my sister, and me—it was the scene of many delicious breakfasts, lunches, *goûters* (snacks), and dinners. The pantry was always filled with necessities such as nuts, dried and canned fruits, jams, cheeses, eggs, milk, cream, butter, all sorts of herbs, garlic, chocolate, teas, and, of course, crusty French bread. That kitchen made a great impression on me and I always refer back to it when designing a kitchen for a client or for myself.

The ritual of the family meal, which once determined the tempo of family life, is for many a thing of the past. This is partially due to the fact that women, who have been traditionally in charge of the kitchen, have joined the workforce. However, recently families have come to realize that having meals together whenever possible is an important part of a well-lived life. All of a sudden the pendulum is swinging back to the ways of my childhood, and a yearning for natural, nutritious, and great-tasting food is strong. The pleasures of a well-prepared meal are now appreciated. Today, the old-fashioned kitchen is, once again, in vogue, yet with modern amenities—a dishwasher, a freezer, and a self-cleaning gas oven. Having the kitchen at the center of family life is considered important. And even the pantry, a practical addition, is back. For a fleeting moment in time, the kitchen was considered dispensable, but this notion has been proven wrong. It is the heart and soul (with or without a fireplace) of a home.

Your kitchen is your domain, and you should feel totally comfortable in it. Make it a place where family and friends enjoy gathering while you (or whoever in your family) prepares the meals. Always be ready for the expected, and the occasional unexpected, guests. You won't be caught off guard if you keep the pantry well stocked with basic ingredients that can be quickly whipped up into a tasty dish. This will make food preparation more manageable.

Remember that cooking is a source of great pleasure for not only the home cook but also those who get to partake in his or her dishes. Well-prepared food stimulates all sorts of emotions, including unlocking personal stories about past eating experiences.

TOP: A wire basket comes in handy to hold fruits and vegetables for a trip to the farmers' market.
BOTTOM: A scale, like this old-fashioned one with copper weights, is a useful kitchen tool.

KITCHEN DESIGN

A KITCHEN IS generally constructed of wood, marble, and/or stainless steel; it's a matter of personal taste. This special space should not only be functional but also offer limitless possibilities for creativity. So no matter what the size of your kitchen, make it as user-friendly as possible. Organization is key to a happy kitchen. Make it work for you.

SETUP

❧ Natural light is key to making a kitchen user-friendly. To compensate for lack of natural light, make sure to have plenty of electrical lighting.

❧ Two sinks are better than one: a deep sink to hide dirty pots, and a second one, space permitting, that is the traditional depth.

❧ Two dishwashers are a major convenience if you entertain frequently. If there is space, this luxury is less expensive than having extra cabinetry built.

❧ It is easier to maintain a tidy kitchen if trash receptacles are built-in and behind closed cabinet doors.

❧ A good oven and cooktop are essential. My preference is for gas instead of electric because gas allows for better control of the heat.

❧ A butler's pantry, once considered old-fashioned, is now in vogue. It is a practical space for storing food. Functionality is key to its design. There is no need to spend the money to make it picture-perfect.

KITCHEN MUST-HAVES

WHEN IT COMES to kitchen equipment, there are endless choices. How many pots and pans do you actually need? Make sure that before you go out and purchase a slew of unnecessary tools, you ask yourself a few questions: What kind of cooking do you do? How many people do you cook for? What are your needs?

Pots and Pans

Good pots and pans with lids will last for generations and make cooking a pleasure. It is best to start off with at least several well-made ones, and if need be to fill in with less expensive ones that can later be replaced.

COPPER COOKWARE
Copper is one of the best heat conductors. It also looks beautiful and lasts forever. Traditionally lined with tin, nickel, or stainless steel to prevent the toxic interaction of the copper with the food, the best copper cookware is thick and heavy. To keep it shiny, clean the outsides with a commercial copper cleaner or with a paste made of vinegar and salt, rinse well, and then polish with a soft cloth.

EARTHENWARE AND STONEWARE
These materials retain heat well but are poor heat conductors. They are recommended for baking or for cooking a gratin the way it has been prepared for centuries. Most will crack if used for stovetop cooking or if exposed to dramatic temperature changes.

ENAMEL COOKWARE
One of the hallmarks of a French kitchen, enamel cookware comes in many colors and combines attractive shapes with durability. Most enamel cookware can also go from the stovetop to the table.

GLASS, CERAMIC, AND PORCELAIN WARE
Easy to care for but not good heat conductors, this type of cookware is best used for baking.

EQUIPMENT

❧ Baskets for storing produce and for gathering from a home garden

❧ Blender

❧ Coffee maker, even if you don't drink coffee (often guests will request coffee)

❧ Food processor, which most cooks, including myself, consider mandatory

❧ Knives (including a stainless-steel or carbon-steel 8-inch chef's knife, paring knife, serrated bread knife, and thin slicing or boning knife) and a steel or whetstone to sharpen them

❧ Salad spinner

❧ Scale for measuring ingredients

❧ Slow cooker

❧ Small kitchen tools: grater, measuring cups for both liquid and dry ingredients, measuring spoons, mortar and pestle, pepper mill, spatula, soup ladle, strainer, tongs, vegetable peeler, wire whisks, and wooden spoons

❧ Teakettle

❧ Toaster

FOOD PRESERVATION AND STORAGE

BEFORE THE INVENTIONS of the refrigerator and freezer, storing and preserving food was a major task. Fruits such as apples, pears, grapes, figs, and tomatoes were dried in the cellar. Meat was dried or cured, and fish was salted or smoked. After harvesting, vegetables were canned or pickled in brine. Potatoes were kept in baskets in the root cellar. These timeless methods are natural ways of ensuring a delicious food supply for the winter months. We can learn a lot from the way our forbears stored and preserved their food supply—and then put our own modern twist on their techniques.

Fresh Fruits and Vegetables

Nothing is better than to eat fresh in-season fruits and vegetables. I do believe that the resurgence of specialty food stores and farmers' markets is helping people understand the value of seasonal and local produce. More and more I find myself buying fruits and vegetables from nearby farms or growing them in my garden. The taste is so much better. When fruits and vegetables are in season, I am often faced with the problem of storing an overwhelming bounty.

The most important rule for preventing produce (either store-bought or homegrown) from going bad is to select perfect specimens. Pick fruits and vegetables that are optimum size. The younger and fresher they are, the longer they will keep. Separate damaged ones and use them immediately. Dispose of anything that looks diseased. The ideal temperature at which to store fruits is around 40°F. Vegetables are best kept in a cool, dark, and dry spot. My grandmother put fruits and some vegetables in a dark room with low humidity that faced east. Following is a list of fresh fruits and vegetables that store well.

APPLES

Ever since Eve took that famous bite out of the forbidden fruit in the Garden of Eden, apples have played a special role in our diet. Although an apple has high sugar content, it is a good source of iron (better than spinach), potassium, and vitamins, and is only about 52 calories. The apple varieties available today (see page 83 for growing) are endless. The best time to buy them is in the fall.

⚜ STORAGE ⚜ Be sure to select firm apples without blemishes or wrinkles, as these will last longer. For optimum storage, place them on a dark shelf in the pantry; an unheated cool garage is a good alternative. Apples should be stored with their stems upright.

Apples can be dried and made into delicious rings that are perfect for snacking (see Drying Method on page 49).

APRICOTS

Tender and juicy, apricots are beautiful orange-colored fruits that are full of beta-carotene. They are also an excellent source of vitamins A (which helps with vision) and C as well as fiber, which has a wealth of benefits including preventing some digestive ailments. I love apricots in all forms—as a fresh fruit, dried, baked in pastry, stewed into a delicious jam, and distilled into brandy and liqueur.

❧ STORAGE ❧ Ripe apricots need to be eaten quickly and should never be refrigerated.

To enjoy apricots when not in season, consider freezing them (see Snap-freezing Fruits and Vegetables on page 50). They need to be halved and pitted first. Another option is to can them (see Canning and Preserving Fruits on page 47).

BANANAS

Bananas release ethylene gas naturally, which causes ripening and enzymatic browning of not only the fruit but also other produce that is nearby. Much of this off-gassing takes place at the stem.

❧ STORAGE ❧ Store bananas in a separate bowl from other fruit on the kitchen counter. To keep bananas more than a week, place them in the refrigerator, but be aware that this may cause the taste to become slightly bland.

FIGS

Did you know that figs are flowers that never open but have instead ripened like most fruits do at the end of the summer? For that reason the fig tree is the only fruit tree that does not display flowers. Thousands of small seeds agglutinate to form the fruit. Another strange characteristic is that only the female figs are edible. One drawback is that figs are not exactly dietetic as they have high sugar content. Besides being one of the sweetest fruits, the fig contains appreciable quantities of vitamins A, B, and C, and it has laxative and digestive properties.

Choosing fresh figs is a skill that can be easily mastered. It is impossible to judge their readiness by color alone. A dark purple color does not necessarily mean that the fruit is ripe. The best way to determine ripeness is by touch: if a fig feels soft, it is ripe.

❧ STORAGE ❧ Always keep fresh figs at room temperature, and only for a couple of days. Since figs are fragile and bruise easily, don't pile them on top of each other. And refrigeration kills their delicate aroma. Figs are best eaten right from the tree.

GRAPES

Best known as the key ingredient in wine, grapes are flavorful and make a wonderful snack or accompaniment to cheese (see Dried Fruits on page 30). This fruit of the vine, which grows in bunches on a stalk, comes in many varieties with green, yellow, black, white, or purple skin enclosing a sweet pulp with one to four seeds. Both the white and black varieties are used to make wine; other varieties are cultivated as dessert grapes. When buying dessert grapes, choose fruit that is clean, ripe, firm, and not too closely packed on the stalk, which should also be firm and crisp. Avoid grapes that are shriveled and damaged. Before they are eaten, grapes should be carefully washed in water with a little bit of lemon juice.

❧ STORAGE ❧ Refrigerate in a Ziploc bag. Or, the old-fashioned way to preserve grapes is to place them stalk first in a pitcher filled with water.

LEMONS AND LIMES

Lemons and limes are citrus fruits that contain unique antioxidant properties. These fruits are also an excellent source of vitamin C. Purchase lemons and limes that are heavy; they have lots of juice. Heavier lemons and limes will last longer and not dry out as quickly as thin-skinned ones.

❧ STORAGE ❧ The best way to keep lemons and limes fresh is to put them in a Ziploc bag in the refrigerator. Or, the old-fashioned way is to place them in a bowl and cover them with fresh water, which should be changed regularly. This storage method, used in Morocco, makes the fruit juicier.

MUSHROOMS

Mushrooms are a delicious fungus—a plant with neither chlorophyll nor flowers that generally grows in cool, damp places where the soil is rich in humus. Despite a high water content, most mushrooms are richer in phosphorus, nitrogenous substances, and vitamin B than green vegetables. And, they are low in calories. Wild mushrooms have been gathered for food throughout history. Identifying them properly is critical as some species are poisonous. If you are not a mushroom expert, purchase mushrooms from the grocery store or at a farmers' market. Edible mushrooms include cultivated species of *champignons de Paris*, which come in two varieties: white and golden (the latter of which is more flavorful), as well as numerous varieties of field mushrooms including boletus, chanterelles, horns of plenty (also known as the black chanterelle), portobellos, mousseron mushrooms, and cèpes.

❧ STORAGE ❧ Use fresh mushrooms as soon as possible to avoid bug infestation. The genus Amanita (which includes many edible mushrooms) or *champignons de Paris* (with the exception of chanterelles and cèpes, which can be refrigerated for up to three days) should be consumed immediately.

To retain the full flavor of mushrooms, do not peel or wash them. Wipe them with a damp cloth or brush them to remove any dirt, and then gently pat them dry. If the stem is tough, remove it. Otherwise, slice off the base of the stem.

Dried mushrooms make a great substitute for fresh mushrooms. Keep a supply in your pantry for use in recipes that call for mushrooms when you don't have time to buy fresh ones.

ORANGES

During the late fifteenth century Italian and Portuguese merchants introduced the sweet orange to the Mediterranean. Considered a

luxury, oranges were often given as gifts. In fact, the French revolutionary Robespierre was described as a sybarite because he served "pyramids of oranges" to his guests. Today in France oranges are the second most popular fruit after the apple. Oranges contain only 44 calories per 100 grams and are rich in vitamin C. When buying oranges, choose specimens that have a shiny skin and some heft.

✦ STORAGE ✦ Oranges can last for 6 to 8 weeks. The secret to longevity is in careful selection. Be sure that none of the oranges you choose are damaged; discard any that show signs of decay. Wrap each fruit individually in newspaper. Place the wrapped oranges in a cardboard box or wooden crate. Store the box or crate in a cool, dark, and dry place where the temperature is maintained constantly at 38°F.

Orange peels can easily be candied and preserved (see Candied Fruits on page 51).

PEACHES

Peaches have been a popular fruit in the American South since the Spaniards first brought them to North America in the sixteenth century. California, Georgia, and South Carolina are the largest producers of peaches in the United States. You can find delicious peaches in Connecticut and on Long Island during the summer. When shopping for peaches, choose fragrant fruits that are unblemished and not overly firm. Because fresh peaches are highly perishable, don't buy more than you plan to use. Even when unripe, they spoil easily. Peaches that are a greenish color were probably picked too early and should be avoided as their sweetness does not increase after picking.

☙ STORAGE ❧ You will be surprised to see how much better peaches will keep if you wrap them individually in newspaper. Place the wrapped peaches preferably in a wood crate. Store the crate in a dark and dry part of your pantry. Do not put them in the refrigerator as the coldness will change their texture.

Peaches will peel more easily if blanched for 1 minute in boiling water, and then plunged in cold water for 1 minute to stop the effect of the heat. They discolor quickly when exposed to the air; sprinkle them with lemon or lime juice if not eating them or cooking with them immediately.

PEARS

There are more than 5,000 varieties of pears. Joining the old-fashioned European yellow pears are crimson-red varieties and small, round Asian varieties. European pears have the traditional bell shape; their flesh is soft and succulent. Asian pears have green-yellow or russet skins and their unique flesh is crunchy. Pears can improve in both texture and flavor after picking. The most popular variety in America is the 'Bartlett', which is available in early to mid-September.

☙ STORAGE ❧ If you are not planning on using pears immediately, select ones with a slightly green skin and allow them to ripen in a cool, dark place. For ideal storage, turn to this old-fashioned method: Leave pears on their stalks and place them stalk down on a shelf in the pantry. Use a drop of wax at the end of the stalk to secure the fruit in place.

QUINCES

The quince is a pear-shaped fruit that turns a bright golden yellow when ripe. The skin of the immature fruit has an odd appearance in that it is covered with fuzz, which rubs off. Quince has a strong, sweet smell and a tart, astringent flavor. It cannot be eaten raw, as its flesh is hard and bitter. Quince is low in calories and rich in tannin and pectin. Pectin is an essential ingredient for making jam and jellies. Use pectin to makes jams, jellies, and quince paste (see Canning and Preserving Fruits on page 47).

⁊ STORAGE ⁊ Store quinces at room temperature until ripe. Then transfer them to the refrigerator, where they will keep up to 2 weeks.

STRAWBERRIES

The strawberry is both refreshing and full of flavor and it contains very few calories. It is low in sugar, a good source of vitamin C, and rich in potassium and other minerals. Strawberries are a delicate fruit that should be eaten right away since they are perishable. They should not be exposed to heat, or handled too much.

⁊ STORAGE ⁊ Keep unripe strawberries for a maximum of 48 hours in the refrigerator, loosely covered with plastic wrap or a towel.

Strawberries should be sprinkled quickly with water and never be soaked.

TOMATOES

Tomatoes are part of the fruit family. There are countless varieties (see page 82). Handle tomatoes gently as they will bruise, in particular the tender part directly around the stem. Be careful not to drop or squeeze them. Keep tomatoes away from major heat sources, such as stovetops and microwaves. Tomatoes should not be placed in direct sunlight unless they need to ripen. If this is the case, line them up on the windowsill, or if there is room, place them on the sill or in a shallow bowl. Move them around gently in the bowl every day to avoid dark spots and bruises, which lead to rotting.

⁊ STORAGE ⁊ One of the most common mistakes is to store tomatoes in the refrigerator. After a couple of days refrigerated tomatoes become mealy and their flavor dissipates. There are far better ways to keep them tasting sweet and to maintain their firm texture. Put the tomatoes in a shallow bowl. If you place them with their stems facing upward, they will stay fresher longer. Temperature is an important factor when storing tomatoes. Room temperature without fluctuation is preferable. Tomatoes stored in the correct way should stay good for up to 1 week.

Dried tomatoes are a wonderful alternative to fresh ones (see Drying Fruits and Vegetables on page 49).

This traditional cheese platter consists of a variety of goat cheeses, blue cheese, Époisses, Camembert, Pont-l'Evêque, and tome (see page 27 for further information about cheese), which have been placed on leaves, and decorated with geranium blossoms. Pair cheese with crusty French bread, sweet seasonal fruit, and a quince paste or fig jam (see Canning and Preserving Fruits on page 47).

Pantry Essentials

A well-stocked pantry is crucial—by always having basics on hand, cooking becomes hassle free. Nothing is more annoying than trying to prepare something at the last minute, realizing that you are missing one key ingredient, and having to rush out to get it. The pantry is the best place to store some fresh fruits and vegetables, along with dried, pickled, and canned produce and other ingredients. However, some essentials, such as butter, cheese, and eggs, need to be refrigerated.

Your pantry can be as rudimentary as a kitchen cabinet, either open or concealed with doors, and should be fitted with lots of shelves. If there is space, create a separate pantry room off the kitchen, or even in the basement or a cool garage. If you are lucky enough to have a pantry room, keep it cool for optimum storage conditions. The pantry can also function as a temporary storage spot over holidays or when the refrigerator or the kitchen garden is otherwise bursting.

BREAD

Always have bread, the basic food staple, in the pantry. Made from a flour-and-water dough with yeast that is fermented, kneaded, and baked in the oven, bread is the only food, along with butter and wine, that is always present on the French dining table. Bread is a traditional accompaniment to most dishes. It is also used for sandwiches, toasts, croutons, and bread crumbs. A good French bread or country-style loaf must have a crisp crust, an attractive golden color, and a soft crumb. Growing stale too quickly is a sign of a tasteless bread. Most bread should be served at room temperature.

❧ STORAGE ❧ Bread can be kept for up to 1 week in a metal or wood bread box. You can also freeze bread (a baguette or a loaf works best). Warm it up in the oven, and *voilà*, you will then have fresh bread!

Bread is best served in a wicker or cane basket, lined with an attractive linen napkin.

BUTTER

A dairy product, butter contains vitamins A and D, calcium, and phosphorus. Its color varies from creamy white to golden yellow according to the cow's diet. A pasture rich in carotene results in a yellow-colored butter. Used in cooking or for spreading on bread and muffins, butter has a delicious nutty taste. It is available salted or unsalted. At room temperature, a good butter should not sweat droplets of water, be sticky, or be brittle.

❧ STORAGE ❧ Butter keeps fresh when refrigerated. Place it in the butter compartment of your refrigerator or in an airtight dish because it easily absorbs odors. Or, the old-fashioned French method of storage is to keep butter in an earthenware container filled with salt water, especially in warm climates. If butter is exposed to light or heat, it will oxidize and become rancid.

Salted butter keeps longer than unsalted butter as the salt acts as a preservative.

CHEESE

Cheese is a highly nutritious food that is enjoyed worldwide. Who could imagine that cheese, like fruits and vegetables, have seasons? The French cheese Vacherin is available during the winter; Époisses and blue cheeses are best between mid-April to mid-November;

while Beaufort, Brie, and Pont-l'Evêque are at their peaks between mid-November and mid-April. Throughout history cheese has been eaten by itself but it is also a key ingredient in cooking. Cheese varies in flavor and texture depending upon the type of milk (ranging from cow and goat to ewe and even buffalo) used in their production. A distinction is made between fresh, fermented, and processed cheeses. This explains the huge variety. France alone has more than 500 kinds of cheeses. Today cheeses are available everywhere and specialty catalogue companies can even send delicious varieties to your door.

Delicious simply eaten with bread, cheese is also called for in many recipes. So make sure to always have some in your refrigerator. I like to serve an array of cheeses on a platter alongside a green salad to guests after the main course. Select at least three or four varieties of soft and hard cheeses such as goat, Camembert or Brie, Roquefort, and either Gouda, Cheddar, or Emmental.

❧STORAGE❧ Store cheeses, loosely wrapped, in your refrigerator's airtight compartment. Be sure to take the cheeses out of the refrigerator at least 1 hour before serving.

Blue cheeses should be slightly damp when serving.

Traditionally, Gruyère is kept in an airtight box with a lump of sugar, which absorbs the humidity.

---

and many virtues were attributed to it. Cocoa (derived from the word *cacahuat*) was thought to appease hunger and thirst, give universal knowledge, and cure sickness. It still does all that as far as I am concerned. Today, cocoa is an internationally traded commodity. The best beans are from El Salvador, Belize, Grenada, Guatemala, Madagascar, Mauritius, Panama, Peru, Costa Rica, Cuba, the Dominican Republic, and Ecuador. The quality and price of the finished products reflect the competitive market. Understand that you get what you pay for.

When first opening a bar or box of chocolate, make sure that there is a chocolaty aroma. Next, check the color, which may vary from a deep auburn to the darkest of browns. Break off a piece of the bar and listen carefully. The crystalline structure of cocoa butter gives the characteristic crisp snap. It should be a good clean break that does not shatter.

❧STORAGE❧ Do not refrigerate chocolate because the humidity will destroy the texture. Dark chocolate can last for up to 1 year if it is protected from dampness and stored in a dark place at a constant temperature of about 64.4°F. It should be placed away from strong odors. Milk chocolate can last up to 6 months in the same conditions.

A small amount of dark chocolate makes for a great teatime snack. It provides a sweet source of energy that doesn't have many calories.

CHOCOLATE

For me, chocolate is a must-have in the pantry for use in baking and cooking, or simply enjoying. According to legend, the cacao tree was the most beautiful tree in the Aztec paradise

COFFEE

The coffee plant originated in Ethiopia and the Horn of Africa, where it grows wild even today. This plant bears small red berries that contain seeds, called coffee beans. The horticultural

PERFECT CUP OF COFFEE

1. Use fresh roasted beans, preferably no more than 1 week old.

2. Grind the beans right before brewing them.

3. Use your favorite brewing method: French press, espresso, or drip. Fresh cold water drawn from a tap that has been allowed to run for a few seconds is best. Bring the water to a boil, but do not overboil it. Wait 30 seconds before adding the hot water for brewing. Brew completely.

4. Warm up the coffee mug or cup before pouring in the coffee.

5. Drink the freshly brewed coffee as soon as possible.

Coffee beans are beautiful to look at but you will compromise the coffee's flavor if you store them in ornamental glass canisters on your kitchen countertop. Doing so will cause them to become stale.

and light in order to preserve their roasted flavor. The beans should not be refrigerated because contact with moisture will cause deterioration. Purchase small quantities of beans—only what you will use in the course of 1 or 2 weeks. Excess ground coffee can keep for a short time in the refrigerator.

CORNICHONS

If you are a fan of pickles, I trust that you've discovered the French cornichons, a small pickled gherkin that is part of the cucumber family. These miniscule sour pickles are not only adorable but also delicious and a must-have for the pantry. They are traditionally served as a condiment for a number of classic French dishes, including pâté.

❖ STORAGE ❖ Make sure to have a couple of glass jars of cornichons in your pantry. They will keep for at least 1 year. Once opened, place the jar in the refrigerator.

propagation and diffusion of coffee began in Yemen. Venetian traders brought coffee to Europe in 1615, tea was first sold in 1610, and the Spaniards brought cocoa from the New World in 1528. Initially coffee was regarded as medicine, much like tea and chocolate.

❖ STORAGE ❖ Correct storage is critical to maintaining coffee's freshness. Store coffee beans in an airtight container placed on a dark shelf in your pantry. It is important to keep them away from excessive air, moisture, heat,

DRIED FRUITS

Raisins, apricots, prunes, cranberries, currants, papaya, and figs are pantry necessities. They make a great snack, go well with tea and alcoholic beverages, and are used in many dishes. Dried fruits have the goodness of fresh fruits but in a concentrated form. High in fiber, dried fruits contain minerals such as calcium and iron, as well as vitamins A and B. Most are very low in cholesterol.

❧STORAGE❧ Store dried fruits in glass, metal, or plastic containers in the pantry. They will keep for up to 1 year.

Some fresh fruits can easily be dried at home, such as apples (see Drying Fruits and Vegetables on page 49).

DRIED HERBS AND SPICES

I love fresh herbs and spices as I feel that they elevate the flavor of most dishes. This is why I not only have a kitchen herb garden but also pots of herbs growing on my kitchen windowsill (see page 55). As fresh herbs are not always available, dried herbs make a good substitute. Herbs that I generally use for seasoning are thyme, rosemary, dill, chives, cilantro, parsley, basil, and bay leaves. My essential spices are pepper, sea salt (see page 39), curry, cumin, ginger, cinnamon, anise, turmeric, and nutmeg. With such a varied assortment, you can make countless memorable dishes.

EGGS

For me, nothing is better than farm-fresh eggs. From breakfast fare to making rich sauces and baking, the egg is an essential ingredient in the kitchen stock. Although the eggs of many birds, or even reptiles, can be used as food, the word "egg" alone applies exclusively to hen's eggs. All other eggs, for example, "quail eggs" or "duck eggs," have to be labeled as such. Eggs are a nourishing and perfectly balanced food that is low in calories (76 calories per 100 grams). They supply all the amino acids essential for the human body and are easy to digest. A fresh egg is heavy and dense. A simple test for freshness is to place the egg in a glass of water. If the egg sinks to the bottom of the glass, it is fresh. If it floats to the top, throw it out. Another way to see if an egg is fresh is to break it on a plate: If the yolk is compact and in the center, it is fresh.

❧ STORAGE ❧ Before the advent of the refrigerator, eggs were stored in a cool, dark spot in the pantry. Today, you need to keep eggs refrigerated. Fresh eggs should be used within 1 month (observe the expiration date) and stored unwashed, with the pointed end down, in the least cold part of the refrigerator.

Do not wash eggs or they will absorb odors.

An egg loses a tiny fraction of its weight every day by the evaporation of water through its porous shell.

To distinguish a raw egg from a cooked egg, spin it. A raw egg turns with difficulty, while a cooked egg is like a spinning top.

GARLIC

An essential ingredient in a variety of recipes, garlic is deeply rooted in history. In sixteenth-century France, it was customary in the spring to eat raw garlic on a tartine to ensure good health. Modern-day researchers have rediscovered that garlic's unique

chemical properties have been shown to lower cholesterol. Today you can purchase dozens of varieties of garlic, from sweet to red-hot. Flavorful gourmet garlic is available in most specialty food stores. Its colors vary from white to various shades of pink and purple to even reddish brown. If garlic's strong odor is a drawback, keep in mind that cooking removes most of the smell. And if you're worried about garlic breath, a handful of fresh parsley eaten after garlic is a good remedy.

❧ STORAGE ❧ Stored in the pantry, garlic can last in the dark for about 6 months (and the pink variety, for up to 1 year). Keeping the garlic's long stalk intact is the ideal method of storage. Braid the stalks together into a long rope, and hang in a cool, dark spot.

Sprouts should be removed from the garlic plant because they make garlic hard to digest.

Quiche au Jambon et Fromage
HAM AND CHEESE QUICHE

SERVES 6

A quintessential French dish, this open-faced savory pie can be made with a variety of delicious fillings. Ham and cheese is the classic but also try my variation.

**One 9-inch store-bought piecrust
(preferably Pillsbury)
¼ teaspoon melted unsalted butter
3 eggs
½ cup freshly grated Swiss cheese
2 slices of ham, cut into small pieces
1 cup whipped cream cheese
1 cup heavy cream (or whole milk)
Optional: ½ cup bacon, cut in small pieces**

1. Preheat the oven to 350°F.

2. Butter a deep 9-inch ceramic pie dish. Place the piecrust inside the dish, and press it into the base and sides of the dish.

3. In a medium-size bowl, thoroughly mix the eggs, Swiss cheese, ham, cream cheese, heavy cream (or milk), and bacon (if using). Pour the mixture into the piecrust.

4. Bake the quiche for about 50 minutes, or until golden. Remove from the oven, and serve warm.

FILLING VARIATION

Pommes de Terre, Jambon, et Poireaux
POTATO, HAM, AND LEEK QUICHE

Add 1 cup of potatoes (boiled and cubed) and 1 cup of leeks (boiled and cut into ½-inch pieces) to the ham-and-cheese filling.

A charming porcelain chicken surrounded by farm-fresh eggs and quail eggs.

GINGER

The root of the ginger plant (*Zingiber officinale*), ginger has a pungent aroma and a peppery sweet taste coupled with a fresh, spicy fragrance. It is of Southeast Asian origin. In ancient China, ginger was widely paired with seafood to counter the fishy odor. In Japan, medicinal qualities are attributed to this root, and many Chinese believe that when eaten, it produces internal warmth that helps to purify the body. That explains why so many green teas are flavored with ginger—it is not only delicious but also soothing. After years of being slighted, ginger is enjoying a new popularity. Whether fresh, pickled, ground, dried, crystallized, or candied, it is no longer restricted to health food stores and Chinese markets.

⁌ STORAGE ⁌ Fresh ginger will keep for up to 2 months if stored in a plastic or glass container in a cool, dry cupboard; crystallized and candied ginger will last much longer.

Ginger mixed with light soy sauce makes a delicious marinade for salmon, tuna, or shrimp. Wrap the marinated fish in aluminum foil and bake in a hot oven for 10 minutes. A lemon ginger and soy sauce dressing for a green salad is equally satisfying. East meets West. Why not?

Serve crystallized ginger or ginger dipped in chocolate as a sophisticated treat at the end of a dinner party. It is excellent for the digestion, too (see Candied Fruits on page 51).

HONEY

It's hard to imagine that a few busy bees are capable of creating such a heavenly substance. I love honey spread on toast for breakfast, added to tea when I'm sick with a sore throat, or as a substitute for granulated sugar in some cookie dough. Manufactured by bees from nectar and stored in the cells of their hive as food, honey is comprised of 20 percent water and 80 percent sugar. Nothing like granulated sugar, the sugars in honey are natural—unrefined glucose or fructose—and easily assimilated by our bodies. The wax and mineral salts, such as calcium, potassium, magnesium, and phosphorous, found in the pollen are also beneficial.

Honey's flavor varies depending upon the season, the species of the flower from which it is derived, and when it is collected from the hive. There is a huge difference between mass-produced blended mixtures of honeys gathered from around the globe and honey from a single type of flower or a specific region. Honey's viscosity ranges from thin to thick—which is better is a matter of personal preference.

⁌ STORAGE ⁌ Jars of honey should be kept on a shelf in the pantry. Liquid honey (the most common form) crystalizes but it will instantly liquefy when warmed up in a bain-marie. Even honey as old as 1,000 years, as was recently discovered at Herculaneum, can still be edible. The moral of the story is that honey will keep for a very long time.

LEGUMES

A variety of legumes, including dried beans, lentils, split peas, and chickpeas, are essential ingredients for your pantry. With them you can make many interesting dishes, including salads, hearty soups, and purees—and feed a small army without spending a fortune.

Legumes are a popular food staple throughout the world, from South America (the black bean in the Brazilian *feijoada*) to North America (the red kidney bean in a Texas chili) to France (the navy bean in a classic cassoulet). They are usually sold shelled and must be soaked for several hours in water before being used (follow the directions on the package).

Beans were first brought to Europe from North America in the sixteenth century. It is believed that Pope Clement VII presented them to his niece, Catherine de Médicis, at her wedding to the future Henri II. They were described at the time as "multicolored red and white seeds, resembling precious stones that might have been lodged in the earth." Precious (and delicious) stones indeed!

❧ STORAGE ❧ Store dried beans in glass containers in the pantry. They will keep for up to 1 year.

MUSTARD

The mustard plant was cultivated in ancient times in Palestine. The Egyptians served its crushed seeds as a condiment. During the Middle Ages, mustard made its way to Gaul where it was valued for its medicinal properties. Pope John XXII (who reigned from 1316 to 1334) was a great aficionado and created a sinecure for his nephew as the post of grand *moutardier du pape* (great mustard maker for the pope). The corporation of vinegar and mustard manufacturers was founded in about 1630 in Dijon. Today, Dijon mustard is prepared with white vinegar. Other mustards are flavored with tarragon, garlic, and fines herbes. This condiment pairs well with charcuterie, is an essential ingredient for a vinaigrette, and is a wonderful component in a marinade for pork, chicken, or fish. Make sure to have an ample supply of mustards in your pantry.

❧ STORAGE ❧ Mustard is best kept in a stoneware or glass jar in the pantry. Once open, store on the bottom shelf of the refrigerator.

NUTS

Squirrels love nuts, and I, too, am nuts about nuts. Squirrels store them for the long, cold winters, and so should you. Always keep nuts in the pantry or the freezer since they make a healthy, filling snack and are used in all sorts of dishes. Nuts run the gamut from walnuts and hazelnuts to pine nuts, peanuts, pistachios, almonds, macadamia nuts, and pecans. Since nuts easily absorb odors from their surroundings, it is important to keep them sealed and separate from other foods.

❧ STORAGE ❧ Due to their high fat content, nuts can go rancid. The best way to store nuts is unshelled in sealed Ziploc bags kept in the freezer. The cold does them no harm; they will keep for up to 8 months. You can also store them in the pantry in tightly sealed glass jars. For unshelled walnuts, fill the bottom of the jar with sand, which will prevent moth infestation.

Almonds

Sweet, dried almonds are primarily used in baking. Recipes for fish (such as trout), chicken dishes, and couscous call for them too.

Cashews

Delicately sweet and crunchy, cashews are packed with antioxidants, minerals, and vitamins. They are delicious salty, too.

Hazelnuts

Hazlenuts are often served on their own. Salted or toasted, they make an ideal appetizer or snack. They are also used whole, grated, or ground in patisseries and confections.

Macadamia Nuts

Macadamia nuts come from Australia (along with the koala). They have an exotic flavor reminiscent of coconut and are primarily used in curry dishes and other stews, and in Asian cooking.

Peanuts

Salted or unsalted, peanuts are a pantry staple, as is a good-quality peanut butter.

Pecans

Pecans are the only nuts indigenous to America. They grow in the northeastern United States and have a taste similar to that of walnuts.

Pine Nuts

Pine nuts, which taste similar to almonds but are slightly spicier, are often browned in a skillet and used in French recipes, including patisseries.

Pistachios

Abundant in Mediterranean countries, pistachios are roasted, salted, and used in cooking poultry and stuffing as well as in sweets, from ice cream to *lokum* (Turkish delight).

Walnuts

A versatile nut, walnuts make an excellent flavoring for sauces to accompany meat and fish, are a fine addition to salads and cheeses, and are a necessary ingredient in many cakes and cookies. They can even be the base for oil, wine, and liquor. To make dry walnuts taste fresh, soak them in milk for several hours before use. I adore macaroons with walnuts (see page 227 for Walnut Macaroons recipe).

OILS

There are several different types of oils for use in cooking. These fats are extracted from trees and plants. Following are my must-haves.

Olive Oil

My favorite oil, olive oil has a distinctive, fruity taste and also is easily digested. An olive oil is graded based on the extraction process used to make it and on the acidity of the pressed oil. Be aware that pressed oil is sold under different qualifications: True extra-virgin olive oil is extracted from olives using only pressure (a process known as cold-pressing) and comes from the first pressing. Considered the finest, it contains just 1 percent acid and has a fresh, fruity flavor. Virgin olive oil also comes from the first pressing, and it has about 3 percent acid. You may also come across the description "light," which refers to the color of oil that has been filtered to remove much of its sediment. "Pure" is a combination of refined virgin and extra-virgin oils. My preference is for Spanish, Greek, and Italian oils. What I look for are extra-virgin oils that are labeled "cold pressed" and produced by a family company or farm.

❧ STORAGE ❧ Store olive oils in glass bottles in the pantry. Most have a shelf life of about 18 to 24 months (check the expiration date on the bottle).

Coconut Oil

Coconut oil is extracted from the coconut. Some claim that it is a superfood owing to its unique combination of fatty acids, which are believed to have a positive effect on one's health. However, many health organizations advise against consuming large amounts of coconut oil due to its high level of saturated fat. It is wonderful in South Asian curries.

❧ STORAGE ❧ Pantry storage is ideal for coconut oil kept in an airtight container or glass bottle. With a shelf life of up to 2 years, coconut oil will transition between solid and liquid states depending on the indoor temperature and season. This will not affect its quality. You can also store coconut oil in the refrigerator but it will turn hard, making it more difficult to scoop or spread.

Walnut Oil

Walnut oil has a distinctive, nutty taste, and is mostly used in dressings or as a seasoning. It has the disadvantage of going rancid quickly.

❧ STORAGE ❧ Store walnut oil in a glass bottle in the pantry. It has a shelf life of about 8 months (check the expiration date on the bottle).

OLIVES

The history of the olive harks back to ancient times in the Mediterranean region, where olives and olive oil were essential components in food preparation. The Egyptians and Greeks consumed large quantities, and the Romans venerated the olive tree, too. There are two basic types of olives: green and black. Green olives are gathered before they are ripe (October in France), and then rinsed and pickled in brine to remove their bitterness. Black olives are harvested when fully ripe (December to January in France). They are then pickled in brine and sometimes in olive oil. Black olives are also dried in the sun. Olives are the main ingredient for many hors d'oeuvres (such as tapenade), a great snack with drinks, and included in many dishes. Therefore, you should have a variety of olives in your pantry.

⚜ STORAGE ⚜ Olives are best kept in glass jars in the pantry. Once open, store in the refrigerator.

ONIONS, SCALLIONS, AND SHALLOTS

What would a kitchen be without the distinct smell and taste of onions (and the hybrids, the salad onion, the scallion, and the small brown-skinned shallot)? They fill out the flavors of almost every type of cuisine imaginable. In fact, onions and shallots, which have a milder flavor, are a staple of French cuisine. Although they may bring a tear to your eye and pungency to your breath, they will also certainly bring delight to your taste buds. The onion, or *Allium cepa*, is on the surface a humble brown, white, or red paper-thin skinned bulb, yet despite its plain looks, it has an intense flavor. Fortunately, yellow onions are available throughout the year. Sweet varieties have a limited growing season and can be found generally only in the spring. Whenever possible, it is best to purchase organically grown onion varieties. Choose ones that have well-shaped outer skins. Avoid those that are sprouting, have signs of mold, soft spots, moisture at their neck, and/or dark patches, all of which may be indications of decay. When selecting scallions, look for those that have green and fresh and crisp-looking tops. The base should be whitish in color for 2 or 3 inches. Avoid those that have wilted or yellowed tops. I am particularly fond of shallots. Cultivated in France at the time of the Carolingians (751–987 CE), shallots closely resemble garlic bulbs—both have heads composed of multiple cloves and are covered with a thin skin. The skin color can vary, from pale brown to pale gray to rose. Choose dry-skinned shallots that are plump and firm without any signs of sprouting or wrinkling.

⚜ STORAGE ⚜ Onions and shallots should be stored in a well-ventilated space at room temperature, away from heat and bright light. Place in a wire hanging basket or a perforated bowl with a raised base so that air can circulate underneath. The length of storage varies with the type of onion. Those that are more pungent in flavor, such as yellow onions, should keep for about a month if stored properly. The sweeter tasting white onion will not last quite as long. Scallions should be stored in a Ziploc bag in the refrigerator, where they will keep for about 1 week. Store shallots in a cool, dry, well-ventilated spot for up to 1 month. As with onions and garlic, do not keep shallots in the refrigerator as they will contaminate the smell of other food.

Onions should be stored away from potatoes, which will absorb their moisture and ethylene gas, causing the onions to spoil more quickly.

POTATOES

The potato is a versatile vegetable. It can be thinly sliced for a gratin, cut in slices to make pommes frites, and boiled in a pot-au-feu. Rich in carbohydrates, vitamins B and C, fiber, and some mineral salts, it is a staple for every kitchen.

⚜ STORAGE ⚜ Potatoes should be stored away from light in a cool, dry, well-ventilated place to prevent them from sprouting. It is important that the storage spot is dark so that

simila, means "flower of flour." It is obtained by coarsely grinding wheat into granules. There are many different kinds: white semolina is ground from rice, semolina for polenta from maize (corn), semolina for kasha from buckwheat, and then yellow semolina is made from wheat and colored with saffron. The nutritional value of semolina is equivalent to that of flour.

❧ STORAGE ❧ Keep grains in glass jars in a cool spot in the pantry. They will last for about 1 year (make sure to check the expiration date on the package).

Rice is extremely versatile. You can whip up inventive rice dishes in no time.

SEA SALT

Throughout the ages salt has not only been revered, it also has been a precious commodity. Many myths are associated with salt. In the ancient markets of the Judeo-Christian civilization—Sumer, Babylon, and Jerusalem—the value of salt was higher than that of gold or incense because salt was thought to bring health and strength. By extension, salt has become a symbol of friendship, and in most societies to this day, sharing bread and salt is the ultimate symbol of peace and hospitality. In Ireland, the land of fairies, it is important to eat salt during wakes to fend off evil spirits. And in Scotland, salt is put in the coffin for the same reason. In Brittany and Italy, it is believed that salt thrown over your left shoulder will ward off evil.

Salt, a minuscule white, grayish, or colorless grain, is sprinkled liberally on food to enhance its flavor. Two basic types of salt exist: rock salt, which is found in a crystalline state in the ground, and sea salt, which is extracted

solanine does not develop—it causes potatoes to turn green and makes them bitter and indigestible.

RICE AND OTHER GRAINS

Every pantry needs a variety of grains, including couscous, quinoa, bulgur, semolina, and at the very least rice. Beloved worldwide, rice is high in dietary fiber. It helps maintain a healthy digestive system and is a good source of vitamin B. There are many different kinds of rice—ranging from brown to Spanish and white—which reached America in the seventeenth century. The Rolls-Royce of them all is wild rice, which is not a true rice but rather the seed of a long black aquatic grass that is native to North America. Rice is generally cooked as a savory dish but sweet concoctions are equally tasty (see page 226 for My Grandmother's Rice Pudding recipe). "Semolina," from the Latin

from seawater by evaporation. The moist, gray-almost-lavender sea salt harvested off the Brittany coast for more than 2,000 years is my favorite. It is the only kind of salt I use due to its delicate taste. Since the sixteenth century this type of salt has been considered one of the world's best. It has a chunky texture and retains the minerals found in seawater: iron, magnesium, calcium, potassium, manganese, zinc, and iodine. These components add flavor. Sodium, the main element in salt, is necessary for humans to have on a daily basis.

❧ STORAGE ❧ Keep sea salt in open ceramic containers on your kitchen counter.

Sea salt and the finer version, *fleur de sel*, are prized by chefs throughout the world. This salt's mild flavor makes it a must for cooking fish, as an addition to butter, or in a dessert to enhance the taste.

Salt is an astringent used for preventing infections and cleaning open wounds; when mixed with vinegar, it is a remedy for snake or bee bites.

If you use too much salt when cooking, you can tone down the effect by adding a raw potato to absorb the excess salt.

TEA

Tea is among the world's oldest and most revered beverages. First discovered in China in 2737 BCE, it was considered a precious commodity, and tea canisters were beautifully decorated. This aromatic beverage, delightful at all hours of the day, is popular worldwide. The first thing that I look forward to is my morning cup of hot tea with a dash of milk. Tea is good for you: it stimulates the nervous system, helps with circulation, and aids digestion. Did you know that all teas come from the same evergreen shrub, *Camellia sinensis*? In the wild the plant can reach a height exceeding 32 feet, but in cultivated plantations, the shrubs are limited to a height of 4 feet so that the leaves can be picked by hand.

❧ STORAGE ❧ To preserve tea's flavor, keep loose tea leaves and tea bags in dry, airtight tins away from direct light. Properly stored, tea will keep for up to 18 months.

How to Make the
PERFECT CUP OF TEA

1. Boil water in a teakettle. Do not use water that has already been boiled.

2. Rinse the teapot with boiling water just before adding a spoonful of loose tea leaves in a tea ball (or as a shortcut, use 1 tea bag).

3. Pour boiling water into the teapot.

4. If using loose tea leaves, the infusion time is 3 to 5 minutes depending on whether the leaves are broken or whole. If using a tea bag, the infusion time is about 3 minutes.

A good quality tea is generally drunk on its own or sometimes with a dash of cold milk. Tea connoisseurs avoid lemon, which denatures the flavor, and often do not add sugar.

VINEGAR
A pantry essential used as a condiment or for cooking, vinegar is a diluted solution of acetic acid obtained by the natural fermentation of wine. The French *vinaigre* literally means "sour wine." This sour-tasting liquid has been produced since Gallo-Roman times. Vinegar diluted with water was a common drink of the Roman legionnaires. There are many different kinds of vinegar. The type depends on the quality of wine or other alcohol used to produce it. Following are my favorites.

Balsamic Vinegar
Originating in Italy, balsamic vinegar is made from aged pressed grapes, not from wine. Historically, it was not oxidized but instead was a type of grape-juice reduction. This artisanal product is prized by chefs and discriminating cooks. Today, to make an authentic balsamic vinegar, grapes are boiled down to a dark syrup, and the vinegar mother starter (*souche*) is added. The mixture is then aged under strict conditions. Most of the balsamic vinegars that you find in the grocery store are a commercial grade, which is made from white vinegar with the addition of coloring from caramel or another sweetener.

Vinaigre Vieux à l'Ancienne (Aged Wine Vinegar)
Obtained by pouring red or white wine into oak casks containing the *souche* (mother starter), this kind of wine vinegar is often aged in the cask and flavored with tarragon, basil, shallot, or garlic.

White Vinegar
White vinegar is industrially made with red or white wine, which has been brewed with beechwood shavings soaked in vinegar for twenty-four hours.

❧ STORAGE ❧ Store vinegars in glass bottles in the pantry. Most vinegars have a shelf life of about 24 months (check the expiration date on the bottle).

PRESERVING THE FRESHNESS OF FRUITS AND VEGETABLES

WHEN I WAS growing up in France, my mother would tell endless horror stories about World War II. One thing that stuck in my mind was that during the long, cold winters, when food was scarce, what was available was not great. Many who were lucky enough to survive the war were terrified of dying from starvation. They developed a strong love of food and a phobia that they might face a shortage of it again. Therefore, when I was growing up, food was appreciated (as it is today) and never wasted. Leftovers were used in a dozen clever ways. Tomatoes and eggplants were stuffed with week-old meat. And bread pudding and French toast, made from day-old baguettes or brioche, were regular treats. My mother's pantry was always amply stocked. There was a surplus of food—almost enough to feed an army. Jars of jams and preserves were piled high, along with jars of cornichons and pickles of all sizes and shapes—depending on what was available in the market or our vegetable garden. Whenever friends or relatives showed up at the last minute, we could always come up with some delicious concoction in a hurry. A few pickles add jazz to cold meat and cheese, and always go well with aperitifs.

Following are my go-to home-canning recipes. Make sure to follow the instructions carefully. When you open a jar of home-canned food, thoroughly inspect it. If it smells bad or is discolored or moldy, throw it out. Otherwise, you may experience food poisoning, or even botulism.

Pickling Vegetables

Pickling is preserving vegetables in a vinegar-based brine, with or without spices. It is one of the oldest ways of dealing with an overabundant vegetable garden. Pickles were as common on nineteenth- and early twentieth-century tables as salads are today, and they served much the same purpose (except that pickles, unlike salads, last a long time). A little crunch and a little sharpness go a long way. Once you master the technique of pickling, it's time for personal experimentation, which is so rewarding. Create interesting twists to the traditional pickling recipes. Think infused beets and dill or small artichokes with lemon rings, or even green tomatoes, onion, and rosemary.

If you plan to serve pickled vegetables within a few days, make them in enamel, glass, stainless steel, or preferably stoneware bowls. Never use copper, brass, or ironware since the vinegar in the brine will react with the metal and change the color of the vegetables. Use sea salt and add some spices. The spices not only enhance the flavor, they also act as a preservative. Malt, wine, white, or cider vinegar should be used. Cider vinegar is more full-bodied and fruitier than white vinegar. Which is preferable is a matter of personal taste. You can also preserve the pickled vegetables in sterilized glass pickling jars. The array of vegetables appropriate for pickling is vast: mushrooms, onions, zucchinis, beets, cauliflowers, unripe tomatoes, cabbages, and even walnuts are all great candidates.

How to Prepare
VEGETABLES FOR PICKLING

1. Select young, underripe, undamaged vegetables.

2. Clean the vegetables (peel them if you like), and then slice or keep them whole. I personally think they look better when kept whole.

3. Soak the vegetables in cold water with ice for 3 or 4 hours, replenishing the ice as necessary. This technique will ensure crispness.

4. Place the vegetables in sterilized glass pickling jars (see Basic Sterilizing Technique on page 47) or a bowl. Pour the brine that has been prepared ahead of time (see page 45 for Classic Vinegar Pickling Brine) over the vegetables. If using jars, screw on the lids afterward.

5. Refrigerate overnight (or up to 2 days).

If the vegetables have been preserved in glass pickling jars, they will last up to a year.

Conserve de Betteraves au Vinaigre
PICKLED BEETS

MAKES ABOUT TEN 16-OUNCE CANNING JARS

This recipe was given to me many years ago by my grandmother and has become one of my must-do annual home-canning recipes. If you have a large amount of beets, make more brine and fill up a few more jars with them.

10 pounds small beets, stems removed
¼ cup whole cloves
1 cup honey
1 quart white vinegar
2 teaspoons sea salt or kosher salt
½ teaspoon fresh-ground black pepper

---

1. Place the beets in a large stockpot and cover with water. Bring to a boil, and cook until tender, about 15 minutes depending on the size of the beets. (If the beets are large, cut them into quarters.) Drain, reserving 2 cups of the beet water.

2. Peel the beets once they have cooled.

3. Sterilize the glass pickling jars and lids by immersing them in boiling water for at least 10 minutes (see Basic Sterilizing Technique on page 47).

4. Fill the jars with the cooked beets. Add several whole cloves to each jar.

5. In a large saucepan, combine the reserved beet water, honey, vinegar, salt, and pepper. Bring to a rapid boil.

6. Pour the hot brine over the beets in the jars, and seal the lids. Then follow the Basic Sterilizing Technique, steps 4 and 5, on page 47.

7. Place the jars of beets on a dark shelf in the pantry to cool to room temperature. Do not disturb them for at least 12 hours.

MAKES ABOUT 4 CUPS

Use this classic brine for pickling a batch
of one kind of seasonal vegetables.

4¼ cups white vinegar
1 cinnamon stick
1 teaspoon whole cloves
2 teaspoons whole fennel seeds
1 teaspoon black peppercorns
1 teaspoon mustard seeds
2 or 3 bay leaves

1. Mix all the ingredients in a large saucepan.
   Bring the mixture to a boil.

2. Transfer to a large bowl, cover with a cloth
   towel, and steep for 3 days in the pantry.

3. Strain the mixture and chill the liquid in a
   container covered with a lid in the refrigerator.
   Use it for pickling.

Like wine, pickles age well in a glass container
or even in an old-fashioned wooden barrel.
They should sit in the brine for 3 or 4 months
or even more before being eaten.

Canning and Preserving Fruits

When the garden is overflowing with fruits such as pears, plums, peaches, berries, figs, or quinces, it is time to make spoon fruits, jams, jellies, and pastes. Serving homemade preserved fruits to your family and friends is a real treat. This is an opportunity to create your own combinations of fruits. I adore lavender and ginger and, when appropriate, add them to my jams. When I am confronted with an abundance of plums, I make a delicious, slightly tart plum jam. It goes with everything—from meat to cheeses to bread and butter.

Canning fruit jams and jellies for the first time may seem daunting but take a deep breath and realize that it is much easier than you think. Note that spoon fruits do not require sterilizing jars; therefore they need to be kept in the refrigerator and eaten within about 3 weeks. Most jams and preserves call for ¼ part underripe fruit (for the pectin) and ¾ part ripe fruit (for flavor and natural sweetness). If you do not have underripe fruit, additional pectin will be necessary. In order to make jams that don't spoil, you'll need to sterilize both the glass jars and their lids in boiling water.

To test the setting point of a jam or jelly, spoon a little onto a cold saucer, and leave it for a few minutes. If a crinkly skin forms when you push it with your finger, it is ready.

If a jam or jelly goes moldy, it means that it was not cooked long enough. Remove the moldy part and cook the leftover again.

BASIC STERILIZING TECHNIQUE
For Jams, Jellies, and Other Preserves, and For Pickling

1. Clean the glass jars, lids, and rings, as well as the utensils that you'll be using, before sterilizing.

2. Place a rack in the bottom of a large stockpot and fill halfway with water. Bring to a boil over high heat. Then carefully lower the clean jars, lids, and rings into the pot using tongs. Leave a 2-inch space between the jars. Make sure that the water covers them by at least 2 inches. Pour in more boiling water if necessary. Bring the water to a full boil, cover the pot, and process for 10 minutes.

3. Carefully remove the sterilized jars, lids, and rings from the canning pot, pouring the excess water from the jars back into the canning pot. Place the jars upright on a towel. Drain the water from the jar lids and rings.

4. Ladle the hot jam, jelly, or other preserves, or place the pickled vegetables into the sterilized jars. Leave ¼ inch of space at the top. Wipe the rims of the jars with a clean towel, and then put the flat lid and ring on each jar.

5. Return the jars to the canning pot full of water. Make sure that the water covers the jars by at least 1 inch. Bring to a boil and boil for 5 minutes to process. Remove the jars and place them on a dark shelf in the pantry to cool to room temperature. Do not disturb them for at least 12 hours.

MAKES ABOUT SIX 6-OUNCE
CANNING JARS

3 pounds strawberries, hulled
1½ cups granulated sugar
3 tablespoon freshly squeezed lemon juice
1 tablespoon fresh lavender on the stalk

1. Sterilize glass jam jars and their lids (see page 47 for Basic Sterilizing Technique). Keep them hot in the canning pot.

2. Put the strawberries and sugar in a medium, deep saucepan. Bring to a simmer, stirring frequently.

3. Pour the mixture into a colander that has been placed over a medium bowl. Gently drain off the juice from the berries into the bowl.

4. Return the juice to the saucepan and bring it to a boil over high heat. Boil, stirring occasionally until the syrup is reduced, about 20 minutes.

5. Return the drained strawberries to the saucepan, and add lemon juice and lavender. Bring the mixture to a simmer. Stir frequently until the mixture becomes jammy. Remove the saucepan from the heat and stir the mixture gently. Ladle the hot jam into the sterilized jars.

6. Follow the Basic Sterilizing Technique, steps 4 and 5, on page 47.

7. Place the jars of jam on a dark shelf in the pantry to cool to room temperature. Do not disturb them for at least 12 hours.

MAKES ABOUT SIX 6-OUNCE
CANNING JARS

I have lots of wild rugosa roses growing in my garden. The rosehips make a delicious jelly.

9 cups raw fresh rosehips
1 package sugarless pectin
2 tablespoons fresh lemon juice
4 cups granulated sugar

1. Wash the rosehips and remove their seeds by slitting them carefully down one side and knocking out the seeds.

2. Place the rosehips in a medium saucepan and cover them with water. Simmer until they become soft, about 10 to 15 minutes.

3. Purée the rosehips in a blender. Combine the puree with pectin and lemon juice.

4. Transfer the puree to a medium saucepan. Bring to a boil. Add sugar and bring to boil again for 1 minute.

5. Follow the Basic Sterilizing Technique on page 47. Ladle the hot jelly into the sterilized jars.

6. Place the jars of jelly on a dark shelf in the pantry to cool to room temperature. Do not disturb them for at least 12 hours.

Rosehips contain tannic acid in their seeds, which causes a chalky taste, so the seeds need to be removed.

Anneaux de Pommes au Four

OVEN-DRIED APPLE RINGS

MAKES ABOUT 4 SERVINGS

4 Granny Smith or McIntosh apples, cored

1. Pre-heat the oven to 150°F.

2. Slice the apples into thin rings. Spread the apple rings on a cookie sheet, making sure that they do not touch each other.

3. Place the cookie sheet in the oven for at least 4 hours until the apple rings are dried out. Flip the apple rings on a regular basis to dry both sides. If you want to speed up the process, increase the heat to 200°F.

4. When the apple rings are done, let them cool on the cookie sheet for at least 20 minutes. Place the rings in a small Ziploc bag, and keep them in a cool dark shelf in the pantry.

   Note: The oven-dried apple rings will keep their taste and color for up to 9 months.

❧

Use this same technique for pears except that once they are dry, you need to flatten them with the back of a wooden spoon.

❧

Drying Fruits and Vegetables

Drying is a popular way of preserving fruits and vegetables. For successful drying, always use good quality, fresh, unblemished produce—bruised fruits and vegetables will rot before they completely dry. Alternately you can buy wonderful dried fruits and vegetables.

This process cannot be hurried. All the moisture must be removed from produce prior to storing it in glass containers either in the pantry or refrigerator. In Provence, tomatoes were often sun-dried for several days. An old-fashioned but relatively simple way to dry grapes is to hang them with a thread secured to their stalk in a light and airy room.

❧

Best fruits and vegetables to dry: apples, apricots, grapes, pears, figs, plums, peaches, mushrooms, peppers, garlic, and tomatoes.

❧

Freezing

Freezing is a relatively easy method for preserving some fruits and vegetables. Most vegetables, except those with high water content, are suitable for freezing. Never freeze produce that has been sitting in the refrigerator for days. It is best to freeze young, fresh fruits and vegetables. Some herbs can be frozen, too (see pages 61–65). The basic method (called snap-freezing) keeps the vegetables in near-perfect condition.

SNAP-FREEZING FRUITS AND VEGETABLES

1. Prepare the fruits or vegetables by peeling and removing seeds (if not desirable). Slice them into uniform shapes and sizes.

2. Blanch the fruits or vegetables in a large saucepan of boiling water for approximately 1 to 5 minutes.

3. Drain the fruits or vegetables and plunge them into ice-cold water. Drain them thoroughly a second time, and seal them in plastic Ziploc bags (making sure to squeeze as much air out the bags as you can). Place the bags in the freezer immediately.

The ideal candidates for freezing are artichokes, asparagus, green beans, broccoli, Brussels sprouts, carrots, cauliflower, eggplant, parsnips, peas, peppers, spinach, sweet corn, sweet onions, and berries.

Haricot Vert Frais, Blanchi
BLANCHED FRESH GREEN BEANS

MAKES 1½ POUNDS OF GREEN BEANS

1½ pounds fresh green beans, with the stem ends snapped off

1. Bring a medium saucepan of water to a boil. Add the beans to the saucepan and bring back to a boil for 1 minute.

2. Drain the beans; plunge them immediately into a bowl filled with ice-cold water. Drain the beans thoroughly a second time, shaking them dry.

3. Seal them in Ziploc bags (making sure to squeeze as much air out of the bags as you can). Place the bags in the freezer immediately.

Onions Doux Congelés à l'Huile d'Olive
FROZEN SWEET ONIONS WITH OLIVE OIL

MAKES ABOUT 12 LARGE SERVINGS

5 pounds sweet onions
2 tablespoons extra-virgin olive oil
Pinch of sea salt

1. Peel the onions, cutting them in half and then lengthwise.

2. In a large sauté pan, sauté all the ingredients, stirring occasionally until most of the liquid has evaporated and the onions are deep golden.

3. Let the onions cool to room temperature. Then spoon them into plastic containers or freezer bags and place them in the freezer.

Note: The onions will keep up to 1 year.

Candied Fruits

Crystallized, glacéed, or candied fruit is perfect for special occasions. The process involves soaking and boiling prepared fresh fruits in a thick sugar syrup for several days. The fruit eventually absorbs a large amount of sugar, which acts as a preservative. Alternatively, wonderful candied fruits are available in specialty food stores.

❧

The best fruits for candying are ginger, lemons, oranges, cherries, and grapefruit, which is my favorite.

❧

Pamplemousse Confit
CANDIED GRAPEFRUIT

MAKES ABOUT 6 CUPS

5 pounds grapefruit
5¼ cups granulated sugar

1. Peel the grapefruit. Cut the peel crosswise into ½-inch-wide strips. As you work, put the strips in a medium bowl full of cold water.

2. Drain the strips and place them in a medium saucepan. Cover the peels with cold water and bring to a boil. Then lower the heat and simmer for 10 minutes. Drain and repeat the blanching process two more times. Cover with cold water again, bring to a boil, then lower the heat, and simmer until the peel is tender, about 30 minutes. Drain in a colander.

3. Add 5 cups of sugar and 5 cups of water to the saucepan. Bring to a boil, stirring until the sugar is dissolved. Then boil without stirring until the syrup reaches 220°F, about 15 minutes.

4. Add the peel and simmer until it is translucent, about 35 to 40 minutes.

5. Remove the saucepan from the heat and let the peel stand in the syrup overnight at room temperature. Bring the syrup mixture to a boil again two more times.

6. Fish out the peel with a fork and arrange the strips on a baking sheet, making sure that they do not touch each other. Put the baking sheet in a turned-off oven to dry for 24 hours.

7. Toss the peels with ¼ cup of sugar, making sure to coat them all over. Set the peels on clean racks to dry again for 1 to 2 hours, then store in an airtight container.

Note: The peels will keep for about 2 months in a metal container with a lid.

Chapter Two

THE
KITCHEN
GARDEN

I was raised to appreciate that cultivating your own herbs, fruits, and vegetables greatly contributes to your well-being. Growing up in Paris and spending time with my family in the countryside—weekends in Normandy and summers in Brittany—I was exposed to the French kitchen garden. This type of planting, which ranges from a humble vegetable plot to an intricately designed garden replete with flowers (known as a *potager*), was brought to an exceptional level during the seventeenth century. The brilliant *jardinier* (gardener) Jean-Baptiste de La Quintinie was responsible for creating some of the most famous kitchen gardens, including those at Versailles, Vaux-le-Vicomte, and Chantilly. The design schemes for these gardens, with their espaliered fruit trees, orchards, cold frames, and irrigation and drainage systems, was imitated throughout Europe. Sophisticated techniques for pruning and transplanting were developed; fragile fruits, such as melon, were grown under hand-blown glass cloches; hearty compost boosted the growth of sweet peas and beans; and white asparagus was protected by straw. These gardening advancements contributed to the growth of culinary delights for the royals. A wall surrounding the garden provided protection and created a microclimate, even during the winter, in which to successfully grow herbs, vegetables, and fruits. The wall was also a means of support for trellises for a variety of climbing crops and it formed a warm backdrop against which fruiting varieties were espaliered. This garden plan led to the creation of the *potager*, a structured space in which vegetables were combined with flowers in decorative patterns. The Château de Villandry in the Loire Valley has one of the most remarkable examples.

To grow your own herbs, vegetables, and fruits is an acquired art, one that brings much pleasure to the gardener who undertakes it. Today's techniques and recipes for preserving herbs, vegetables, and fruits hark back to the past, when herbs were valued as much for their medicinal powers as for enhancing culinary dishes. For example, garlic was used to ward off the common cold. Fruits and vegetables were equally enjoyed, and it was understood that they contributed to a healthy diet. Botanists and gardeners knew that a balanced kitchen garden should include herbs, fruits, and vegetables, and sometimes flowers, too.

Those who possess the gift of making everything grow in the garden have what is known as a green thumb. Gardeners of the past figured out how the moon, sun, and rain impact the soil. They also understood where to plant herbs,

Bring your herb garden indoors. Set pots of basil, chives, and rosemary on the windowsill or on a nearby surface.

fruits, and vegetables in the garden, which plants need to be separated, and how the proximity of certain plants to others can make them flourish. For example, for an optimum crop of tomatoes, plant basil nearby. Such essential and timeless French planting guidelines and traditions have been passed down through the centuries.

Let me share with you my knowledge of and experience with the kitchen garden. You do not need to have acres of farmland or a grand estate. Instead, you can create an ample kitchen garden in a small backyard or terrace, or even consider designing an attractive container garden in a tiny space. The satisfaction that a garden brings is a profound joy no matter what its size.

GARDEN ESSENTIALS

GROW ONLY HERBS, vegetables, and fruits that are recommended for your climate. Make sure to plan your garden carefully since haphazard planting will rarely give good results. Prior to planting, rid the plot of weeds and then prepare the soil well with organic matter. Spread mulch, such as clean straw, sawdust, or peat moss, between the planting rows to a depth of four inches. Mulch will deter weeds from coming up and prevent the soil underneath from drying out. It will also keep the soil loose. Spray plants regularly with a garden hose.

Bees are essential for a successful garden. They carry pollen from one flower to another, help with the cross-pollination of plants, and contribute to the production of fruits and seeds. However, do not expect perfection. Accept that some of your crops may become slightly damaged or even be eaten by predators. Instead of eradicating pests with chemical sprays, encourage birds into the garden to create a biological balance. If they become a nuisance, you can ward them off with scarecrows. Besides, scarecrows can look charming. A well-planned garden design will help to control the spread of disease and the pest population. But the most effective way to prevent blight is simply to grow strong, healthy plants.

❧

Sprinkle a little fertilizer on mulch to help it decay so that it can be used in next year's soil.

❧

What to Feed Your Garden

Plants, just like people, need food in order to grow strong. Plant food is called fertilizer. The time to fertilize is when you are preparing the soil for the garden. The best fertilizer is rotted (e.g., more than 1-year-old) manure. It contains most of the nutrients a plant needs: nitrogen, which helps green leaves to grow; phosphorus, which abets root and fruit development; and potassium, which makes vegetables tender. If you purchase manure, choose rotted cow or horse manure, which won't burn the tender roots of vegetables as chicken or sheep manure would. You may also substitute compost for rotted manure or buy dry or processed manure.

Lime is usually added to soil that has a low pH, the chemical symbol used to express the acidity or alkalinity (sweetness) of the soil. It is measured from 0 to 14, with the middle number 7 being neutral; 0 to 7 is acidic, and 7 to 14 is alkaline. Most vegetables do best in a slightly acidic soil (with a pH between 6 and 7). By adding lime to acidic soil, you raise the pH and help the fertilizer to release its food. By adding aluminum sulfate to sweet soils, you can lower the pH. To test your soil, dip a strip of litmus paper (available at the garden center) into a cup of moistened soil. The paper changes color depending on the pH: If the soil is acidic, the paper will turn red. If it is alkaline, the paper will turn blue.

To prevent garden-tool blades from rusting, wipe the metal regularly with a cloth that has been dipped in oil. To fix a rusty blade, run a sliced onion sprinkled with sugar across its surface.

Put rakes away with the prongs against the ground to prevent an accident. Prongs can hurt.

ESSENTIAL GARDEN EQUIPMENT

- Spading fork and spade to turn the soil
- Rake for the removal of stones, roots, and so on
- Hand cultivator for gently working the soil and keeping the soil weed free
- Garden trowel
- Shovel to dig soil
- Hoe to open planting rows for seeding
- Pruner for trimming and cutting
- Cutting shears
- Yardstick for measuring the length and width of your garden
- String to create straight planting rows
- Wood stakes to mark both ends of each planting row
- Water-resistant marker to write the names of herbs, fruits, and vegetables on stakes or labels
- Watering can and a hose with a sprinkler
- Garden gloves to protect your hands
- Garden boots or shoes
- A basket for gathering your harvest

CREATING AN HERB GARDEN

TRADITIONALLY PLANTED IN a separate space in the garden, herbs are among the easiest plants to grow. Three-quarters (or at least half) of the site needs to be sunny. Most herbs require a slightly alkaline soil with good drainage. Insects don't bother them; apparently the fragrances that are so delightful to us smell awful to them. Herbs are virtually immune to plant diseases as well.

Early civilizations compiled medical and mystical treatises about the sacred properties of herbs, which were also employed to flavor food, as beauty treatments, in celebrations, and in craft making. The recognition of a large number of herbs continued through Greek and Roman times and into Europe. In 812 Charlemagne ordered that a list of herbs be grown on all imperial farms throughout his empire. So, be like Charlemagne, who is known to have said, "Herbs are the friend of physicians and the praise of cooks." The herbs that fulfill most of my cooking needs are basil, chives, coriander, dill, lavender, mint, parsley, rosemary, sage, and thyme. I like to add nasturtiums, an edible flower, into the mix.

When picking herbs, do not just clip the leaves. Instead, cut them from their stems.

Fresh herbs elevate a simple dish.

BASIL {*basilic*}

BOTANICAL NAME: *Ocimum basilicum*

The word "basil" derives from the Greek *basilikos*, meaning "royal." Only the sovereign (*basileus*) was allowed to cut it. This explains why French chefs sometimes call it *l'herbe royale*. In fact, the sixteenth-century British herbalist John Parkinson wrote, "The smell of basil is so excellent that it is fit for a king's house." Basil has a long and honorable history that goes back thousands of years. In Roman times, it was a fixture in the kitchen garden. The Hindus regarded it as a plant that honored Vishnu and Krishna. In Italy basil is associated with courtship. A young girl would set a pot of basil in the window to signal her lover that she was ready for his visit. In fact, even today the herb is referred to as "Kiss me, Nicholas" (*Baccia, Nicolo*). In the Italian countryside when a young man calls on his girlfriend, he sometimes will place a sprig of basil behind his ear to show his fidelity. In Elizabethan England, dried basil was used as snuff to alleviate headaches. Basil eventually made its way to North America in the early seventeenth century and became a favorite herb of the American colonists. There are many varieties used for different purposes—from landscape plants and healing to cooking. In my opinion the best culinary basils are the sweet basil, with its large aromatic leaves, which have a strong clove scent; dwarf basil (*Ocimum minimum*), which has either green or purple leaves; and Italian basil (*Ocimum crispum*), which has curly leaves.

Basil, a hardy plant that can grow 18 to 24 inches high, is one of the first signs of spring. It is easy to grow from seed since germination takes a mere 6 days and requires only water and a sunny spot. The blossoms—small white and sometimes purple flowers—shouldn't reach full bloom because they weaken the plant and dry up the aromatic oils. So be sure to pinch off the buds before they open.

You can't go wrong with basil in a spring or summer salad; it is delicious, especially with tomatoes. For Provençal tomato-based recipes, the French always add basil and garlic. Basil pesto makes a wonderful base for many dishes.

The best way to have fresh basil on hand all year round is to finely chop it and freeze it in an ice-cube tray covered with plastic wrap.

Place pots of fresh basil in sunny windows to quell winter blues.

Add chives to dishes at the last minute. Otherwise the flavor of the herb will be lost.

To preserve chives, finely chop them and freeze the small pieces in an ice-cube tray covered with plastic wrap.

CHIVES {*ciboulette*}
BOTANICAL NAME: *Allium schoenoprasum*
Chives are part of the onion family. The seventeenth-century British botanist Nicholas Culpeper said that this herb does "somewhat provoke appetite, increase thirsth, ease the belly . . ." The flowers are lavender-colored pompons, the leaves are slender and dark green, and the stalk is grasslike. Chives are believed to help with the digestion of fatty food.

This hardy perennial, which reaches 8 to 10 inches in height, is best grown from plants rather than seeds. To retain the stem's flavor, be sure to trim off the flowers. Chives do well indoors.

CORIANDER OR CILANTRO {*coriandre*}
BOTANICAL NAME: *Coriandrum sativum*
A native of southern Europe and the Middle East, coriander is also known as cilantro. The Romans brought this herb to northern Europe. It was used along with cumin and vinegar as a preservative. Medicinally, coriander leaves aid digestion, reduce flatulence, and stimulate appetite.

Coriander is a leafy herb, which grows up to 2 feet in height. Its tall stems are topped with delicate white flowers. The seeds should be sown in the spring. Plant the herb in a sunny area of the garden. The soil needs to be rich and moist.

Fresh coriander leaves are delicious with fish, shrimp, or salad. Dried coriander seeds are also used in cooking and baking. I like to sprinkle them on desserts, in particular cookies.

Freeze coriander to preserve its flavor.

DILL {*aneth*}

BOTANICAL NAME: *Anethum graveolens*

Remains of this ancient plant have been found in Roman buildings and Egyptian pyramids going back more than 5,000 years. The poet Virgil called dill a "pleasant and fragrant plant." The seeds function as a stimulant. In fact, when Sunday sermons were long, church-goers nibbled on the seeds so they would not fall asleep. Dill also aids digestion.

An annual, dill can easily be grown from seeds; germination takes 10 to 12 days. This herb, which reaches a height of about 3 feet, needs full sun, and it thrives in a wide range of soil, conditions, and climates. Cut off the flower heads and dry them in the sun. After drying, gently shake the seeds out and store them in an airtight jar. Note that the plant's foliage is also edible.

Dill seeds are primarily used in cooking and for pickling.

Crushed dill seeds steeped in hot water make a nail-strengthening bath.

GARLIC {*ail*}

BOTANICAL NAME: *Allium sativum*

A member of the onion family, garlic is one of the most widely used herbs. It produces a circular flower head on top of a slender stalk. The ancient Greeks and Romans held garlic in high esteem due to its curative properties. Hippocrates, the most celebrated physician of antiquity and considered the father of modern medicine, classified it as a "sudorific medicine" (sweating medicine).

Relatively easy to grow, this perennial herb should be planted in a sunny spot in rich soil with good drainage. Garlic needs to be watered often during the summer months, or if the climate is hot. In the late summer the bulb's stem and leaves will lose their green color and become limp. This is the time to carefully dig the bulbs out of the ground and then to dry them indoors. Hang them in bunches in a drafty place. During the winter, plant a few of the sturdy outer cloves of a dried garlic bulb (at a depth of 1 inch) in a large pot or container inside. Space the bulbs about 6 inches apart. Make sure to place the pot or container where there is plenty of sunlight. Three garlic plants will produce an ample supply that, for the home cook, should last about 4 months.

LAVENDER {*lavande*}

BOTANICAL NAME: *Lavandula angustifolia*
(English lavender)

There are many cultivated lavender species. I am particularly fond of English lavender as its flavoring is somewhat sweeter than the others. Lavender oil has strong antibacterial properties and a heavenly smell. According to Nicolas Culpeper, who wrote about the herb in 1653, lavender is "of good use for problems of the head, colds, sluggishness, and cramps. It strengthens the stomach and frees the liver and spleen from obstructions." Today lavender is used primarily in aromatherapy and in cooking. Try flavoring ice cream, teas and lemonade, cakes and cookies, salad, and sugar with this versatile herb.

Lavender grows well in most climates but is not resistant to cold temperatures. It requires a sunny spot in the garden and well-drained soil. Practically pest and disease free, its fragrance attracts bees, birds, and butterflies. Lavender is at home as an accent garden plant—trained into a hedge, grown in a border, or hanging over a rock wall. If you have a sunny window, it also makes a lovely houseplant.

Use fresh lavender blooms in bouquets. Or, dry the flowers for wreaths or sachets to place among clothes or in closets to add fragrance and to help deter moths (see pages 130 and 134 for how to make a sachet).

LEMONGRASS {*citronelle*}

BOTANICAL NAME: *Cymbopogon citratus*

Lemongrass is a plant native to India. This warm-climate (at least Zone 9) plant that has the appearance of a patch of tall grass reaches from 3 to 6 feet in height. If grown indoors, it does not achieve this great height. There are two kinds of lemongrass: East Indian and West Indian, which are very similar. Their bulb, or the bottom part of each stalk, and sometimes the leaves, are used in cooking.

Lemongrass tea, which is usually brewed with leaves, can help settle an upset stomach and ease a cough.

For cooking, lemongrass is best used fresh.

Lemongrass acts as an excellent repellent for ants and mosquitoes.

MINT {*menthe*}

BOTANICAL NAME: *Mentha spicata*
(spearmint), *Mentha piperita* (peppermint)

A ninth-century writer remarked that there are as many varieties of mint "as there are sparks from a Vulcan furnace." In my opinion, spearmint and peppermint are the most versatile. Peppermint has the stronger flavor.

Mint is a hardy perennial. Spearmint grows to about 18 inches and produces tiny white flowers, and peppermint grows somewhat taller and produces tiny red flowers.

The plants propagate themselves through underground stems or runners. They can spread so rapidly as to become a nuisance. The best option is to keep mint in a separate, partially shaded area of the garden, or to plant it in pots. Mint takes a lot of nourishment from the soil, which should be moist and well drained. Feed the soil with compost at least twice a year.

Hot mint tea relieves headaches and increases concentration. Steep torn mint leaves in boiling water.

NASTURTIUM {capucine}

BOTANICAL NAME: *Tropaeolum majus*
The word "nasturtium" comes from the Latin word *tropaeolum* which translates "to twist the nose," owing to its peppery aroma. Originating in South America, nasturtium was introduced to Europe in the eighteenth century. Versailles's kitchen garden includes this edible flower. The French still use both the leaves and the flowers to create decorative salads. Nasturtium is high in vitamin C.

This self-seeding edible flower is popular throughout the world. With its brilliant-colored bell-shaped flowers in shades of yellow, orange, and red, nasturtium also makes a beautiful garden border. It is easy to grow and will thrive in poor or even sandy soil.

You can make a satisfying tea by steeping the peppery-flavored flowers in boiling water.

PARSLEY {persil}

BOTANICAL NAME: *Petroselinum crispum*
Parsley, one of the most widely used herbs, harks back to ancient times. The Romans wore parsley crowns at banquets because it was believed to absorb wine fumes and prevent the wearer from getting drunk. It was also believed to cure baldness if the ground-up seeds were sprinkled on a man's head three nights every year. Parsley is high in nutritional value, containing vitamins A, B, and C, iron, and calcium. It is about four times as rich in vitamin C as oranges.

This hardy biennial is usually grown as an annual because the leaves are crisp only during the first year. Parsley can be difficult to grow, partially due to its long germination period of 3 to 6 weeks. To mark the planting row in the garden, mix in a few radish seeds. Partial shade is best.

Parsley freezes well and can be used straight from the freezer. Instead of chopping the frozen leaves, just crumble them.

ROSEMARY {*romarin*}

BOTANICAL NAME: *Rosmarinus officinalis*

Rosemary means "rose of the sea" because the herb originally grew wild on the Mediterranean coast in the salt spray. This perennial has always been valued for its medicinal properties. The ancient Greeks believed that rosemary strengthened the brain and memory. Pliny recommended it for failing eyesight and jaundice. Rosemary was introduced to France and England by the Romans and has flourished there ever since. Cleaning one's face with rosemary boiled in white wine was thought to contribute to a fair complexion. In fact, it is still used today in many hair and cosmetic products. The herb is also appreciated in the kitchen, combining well with pork and lamb, and equally delicious with tomatoes, zucchini, and broiled fish. I use it to make fragrant biscuits.

An aromatic shrub with a pungent flavor, rosemary's pine-like leaves are used either fresh or dried. Rosemary is easier to grow from a cutting than from seeds. The plant makes an elegant indoor topiary.

❦

Drying is the best way to preserve rosemary for use during the winter months.

—

Infuse fresh rosemary leaves in boiling water to make a mouthwash for sweet-smelling breath.

❦

Petit Gateaux au Romarin
SMALL ROSEMARY COOKIES

MAKES ABOUT 30 SMALL SHORTBREADS

These savory shortbreads are ideal for appetizers, because they can be baked a day ahead of serving. Be sure to place them in an airtight metal container and store at room temperature.

2 cups all-purpose flour
4 teaspoons baking powder
½ teaspoon fresh rosemary, finely chopped
2 tablespoons unsalted butter
1 cup whole milk

—

1. Preheat the oven to 350°F.

2. In a medium-size bowl, sift together the dry ingredients. Add the rosemary. Cut in the butter and add the milk.

3. Form the dough into a long roll (about 1 foot long and 2 inches in diameter) and place onto a baking sheet lined with parchment paper. Bake for 20 minutes, or until pale golden. Transfer to a wire rack and cool to room temperature. Slice into ½-inch thick pieces, and serve on a platter.

SAGE {sauge}

BOTANICAL NAME: *Salvia officinalis*

Sage is also known as "salvia," from the Latin *salveo*, which means "I save." There are more than 700 species of this pungent herb. Before the introduction of tea from China, the English drank sage tea. Sage is good for digestion and is used to treat the common cold.

Sage is a hardy medium-size perennial with gray-green foliage. It can grow up to 3 feet in height. The plants need a sunny location.

The best way to preserve sage is to harvest it in large bunches, dry out the leaves, and store them hanging in a dry basement.

THYME {thym}

BOTANICAL NAME: *Thymus vulgaris* (English thyme), *Thymus fragrantissimus* (French thyme)

There are countless varieties of thyme. From a select list of thirty, I chose for my kitchen garden the bushy green English thyme and the gray, narrower-leaved French thyme, because they are flavorful and easy to grow. Since ancient times, this herb has been used as a curative for lung ailments. Thyme has protective properties, and during medieval times its essential oil, thymol (or the plant's ashes), was applied to the skin to counteract the effects of the bites of venomous beasts and insect stings. Thyme is associated with courage. An infusion of this herb to bathwater reinvigorated tired soldiers.

Thyme is easy to grow in either the garden or in a pot on the windowsill. This perennial grows to a height of about 12 inches. Germination takes about 10 days. Rich soil and plenty of sunshine are the only growing requirements. A harsh winter can kill the

How to Make a
BOUQUET GARNI

Add flavoring to your cooking with a classic bouquet garni. A French term, *bouquet garni* refers to a small bundle of herbs, which when simmered in a dish, gently infuses it with mild, aromatic flavor. Add a bouquet garni to soups, stews, or braises. Remove it before serving.

4 sprigs fresh thyme with long stems

4 sprigs fresh flat or curly parsley with long stems

1 bay leaf

Tie the bunch of herbs securely together with kitchen twine, or wrap them in cheesecloth to form a sachet.

plants but sprinkling a packet of seeds during the spring easily fixes this problem. Some creeping varieties, which also can be used in cooking, such as caraway-scented *Thymus herb-barona* and the lemon-scented *Thymus serpyllum*, look attractive between flagstones. When you step on these plants, a delightful pungent aroma is released. This hardy herb will grow almost anywhere except in shady and damp spots. Once established, the plants will spread themselves and self-seed.

Thyme, with its strong pungent flavor, is one of my favorite culinary herbs. Fresh thyme can be used in many dishes, from roast beef to fish, chicken, salad, and eggs. Keep in mind that this herb should enhance the natural flavor of food, not overwhelm it.

Put thyme inside clothes chests to keep out moths—it smells much better than mothballs.

CREATING A KITCHEN GARDEN

A KITCHEN GARDEN measuring 12 feet wide and 12 feet long is large enough to produce plenty of vegetables and fruits for the home cook. The term "kitchen garden" implies a garden that it is within easy access of the kitchen door, enabling the cook to dash out and pick what is needed for a meal. This type of garden (also known as a vegetable patch or plot) is traditionally set in the backyard.

A well-planned kitchen garden should be sustainable. Initially, a soil enricher, such as manure, may be needed to increase the soil richness and improve its texture. The garden should be located in a sunny spot that is sheltered from wind. Make sure to take into consideration the following prior to planting:

⊰ Adequate soil drainage is essential. To test the ground, dig a hole about one foot deep and fill it with water. If the water is retained for more than thirty minutes, you need to take corrective steps. One option is to move the location. The other option, which is inexpensive, is to create raised beds.

⊰ Composting is an essential requirement for healthy soil. Set aside an area within the garden for composting. Use this spot to plant once the compost heap has broken down and begin a new pile in another spot. This labor-saving method ensures that all areas of the garden will be rich in nutrients.

⊰ Construct a garden wall. It will provide additional warmth and thus extend the growing season. The wall will also serve as a support for climbing vegetables such as pole beans and cucumbers.

The following vegetables and fruits are my favorites. Note, in my opinion, some require so much work to grow at home that you may choose to buy them at the farmers' market.

Vegetables

ARTICHOKE {artichaut}
BOTANICAL NAME: *Cynara scolymus*
The artichoke is a perennial whose edible immature flower head is formed of a heart-shaped base surrounded by leaves. The artichoke is a variety of the thistle species that has been cultivated as food. Originating from Sicily, the artichoke was initially regarded by the French as a remedy for various ailments, such as phlegmatic and melancholic dispositions. This vegetable not only has diuretic properties, it also is rich in iron and potassium and low in calories.

Since the artichoke needs a sizable amount of space in a garden, I suggest buying it rather than growing it. Although available year round, it is best in the summer.

ASPARAGUS {asperges}

BOTANICAL NAME: *Asparagus officinalis*

The asparagus is a member of the lily family; the most popular varieties are white and green. A native of the eastern Mediterranean region and Asia Minor, asparagus was known to the Egyptians and Romans but not cultivated in Europe until the time of Louis XIV. The Sun King was particularly fond of this vegetable. Long valued for its medicinal properties, asparagus is reputed to help eyesight, soothe toothaches, and cure the effects of insect stings. Rich in vitamins A and C and low in calories, asparagus also has diuretic qualities.

Asparagus can be grown from seeds, but usually 1-year-old plants are planted in the garden. I prefer to buy asparagus, which is tricky to grow, at the farmers' market.

BEANS {haricots}

BOTANICAL NAME: *Phaseolus coccinus* (climbing, or pole, beans), *Phaseolus vulgaris* (French beans)

Climbing and French beans are often grown for their decorative appearances. They both like well-drained soil in a sunny spot. If planted in a window box, they make an attractive leafy screen that diffuses sunlight. They are also delicious and grow quickly. There are many varieties of beans; all are easy to grow.

Since beans will not germinate in cold ground, the first sowing should be in the spring when the danger of frost has passed. A second sowing should be done in late summer or autumn. Each seed needs to be planted in the soil at a depth of two inches. Plant seeds in a sunny area where the soil drains well. Harvest beans when young and tender as this will encourage further production.

VINAIGRETTE

MAKES ⅔ CUP

This basic vinaigrette is perfect for dressing a tossed green salad, asparagus, artichokes, and other vegetables. For an alternative flavor, try adding lemon juice, garlic, and fresh herbs. The vinaigrette, stored in a glass container, will keep for several weeks. I always keep vinaigrette in my pantry, and I like to add a clove of garlic, a basil leaf, or some stalks of fresh herbs to the glass jar—they infuse the oil with a wonderful flavor.

1 tablespoon mustard
1 tablespoon red wine vinegar
4 tablespoons extra-virgin olive oil
Sea salt and freshly ground pepper to taste
Optional: 2 stalks of fresh thyme or rosemary, 1 clove of garlic, or 1 basil leaf

1. In a small bowl, whisk together the mustard, vinegar, and oil. Season with salt and pepper.

2. Pour the vinaigrette into a glass jar with a lid, and store, covered, in the pantry.

Note: Never refrigerate vinaigrette.

BEETS {betterave}

BOTANICAL NAME: *Beta vulgaris*

Enjoyed since ancient times, beetroot was described by the French soil scientist Olivier de Serres in 1600 as "a very red, rather fat root with leaves like Swiss chard, all of which is good to eat." Rich in sugar, vitamins, and calcium, beetroot can be eaten raw or cooked. In my opinion, the best way to prepare beets is to bake them in the oven. They can also be

pickled. Use the leaves in soups or prepare them like spinach.

Beets are easy to grow in a wide range of climates. Sown from seeds in early spring to late summer, and even into autumn in warmer climates, the young plants should be spaced 6 inches apart in the vegetable plot. They will need to be thinned out as they grow. Prevent weed growth around them. Choose a beet such as 'Early Wonder' or 'Detroit Dark Red' and you will have beets six to eight weeks after planting.

BROCCOLI {broccoli}
BOTANICAL NAME: *Brassica oleraceavar var. italica*

Broccoli is part of the cabbage family; there are green, white, and purple varieties. Originating in Italy, broccoli was introduced to France by Catherine de Médicis. For Italians, broccoli is a favorite spring vegetable, often cooked with olive oil and garlic.

Broccoli grows well from seeds or seedlings. It does not require a very rich soil, and it is a good crop to follow peas or beans in a crop rotation. An open sunny area and good drainage are essential. Broccoli is harvested 10 to 12 weeks after the seeds have been sown.

BRUSSELS SPROUTS {choux de bruxelles}
BOTANICAL NAME: *Brassica oleracea var. bullata*

Brussels sprouts are cultivated for their green buds, which resemble tiny cabbages. The sprouts are rich in sulfur, potassium, and vitamins.

A cool-to-cold climate is necessary for the growing success of Brussels sprouts. Plant them in rich and well-drained soil. Soil that has been manured for a previous crop is preferable to freshly manured soil. This vegetable

takes from 5 to 6 months to mature. When they are ready, cut the buds off the base of the main stem with a knife. Note that the sprouts are prone to attacks by white cabbage moths and cabbage butterflies.

I use laundry bar soap (such as Fels-Naptha or Zote), which can be purchased in most hardware stores, to protect Brussels sprouts from cabbage moths and butterflies.

CABBAGE {choux}
BOTANICAL NAME: *Brassica oleracea var. capitata*

Wild cabbage, from which all the cultivated varieties are derived, is a perennial with broad leaves. The different varieties of cabbage are distinguished by their colors (white, green, red), their shape, and leaf texture (crinkly or smooth). Known for more than 4,000 years in

The seeds of carrots are very small, making them difficult to sow. Plant them in shallow drills covered with light soil, or scatter them thinly in well-prepared beds. Carrots need a light well-drained soil. Young carrots can be harvested progressively, starting with small roots. Allow some to grow larger but not too large as they will split, especially in wet weather. Plant 'Scarlet Nantes' or 'Royal Chantenay'.

Carrots should not be scraped or peeled but instead brushed under cold water because the vitamins are concentrated in the skin.

Use the carrot's green top when making a soup stock.

CUCUMBER {concombres}

BOTANICAL NAME: *Cucumis sativus*

The cucumber originated in the foothills of the Himalayas, where it grows wild. Pliny recounts that the Romans and Greeks were particularly fond of cucumbers. In France they were eaten during the reign of Charlemagne. Jean-Baptiste de La Quintinie cultivated the cucumber under cover so that it could be served at Louis XIV's table as early as March or April—a luxury at the time. There are several varieties of cucumbers including some that are seedless. Ninety-six percent water and low in calories, the cucumber contains minerals and vitamins A and C.

Sow the seeds directly where the plants are to be grown. They have a tendency to spread a lot so try to keep them high on a trellis. Add plenty of manure or compost for a successful crop. Pick cucumbers when they are young and fresh. If left too long, they will become tough and bitter.

Europe, cabbage was first valued for its medicinal properties. Low in calories, this vegetable is rich in mineral salts and vitamins.

Cabbage can be grown in all climates throughout most of the year. Pick a mature cabbage when its heart feels firm and plump. Avoid leaving cabbage in the ground too long as it will become tough. Protect this vegetable from snails and moths (see pages 90-91 for two green methods).

CARROT {carottes}

BOTANICAL NAME: *Daucus carota*

Carrots, grown mostly for their orange-red edible root, are one of the most popular vegetables in France, after the potato. The ancients recognized that carrots are good for eyesight. The carrot has a high water content and is rich in sugar, mineral salts, and vitamin A. It also contains a pigment called carotene.

EGGPLANT {aubergine}

BOTANICAL NAME: *Solanum melongena* var. *esculentum*

Originating in India, the eggplant was cultivated in Italy by the fifteenth century and spread to the South of France in the seventeenth century. The vegetable comes in purple and in white. Eggplant is high in potassium and calcium.

This trouble-free plant is easy to grow. It is best to start with seedlings and transplant them into the garden when the soil has warmed up and all danger of frost has passed. Staking is necessary to support the plant when it is in fruit as it has a tendency to spread a lot.

LEEKS {poireaux}

BOTANICAL NAME: *Allium ampeloprasum*

Leeks were cultivated by the Egyptians and the Hebrews. The Romans believed that the vegetable helped maintain one's speaking voice. Low in calories, the leek is rich in vitamin A, sulfur, and other mineral salts, and it is a good source of dietary fiber.

Leeks need a rich soil. Plenty of well-rotted manure should be added prior to planting.

LETTUCES {laitues}

BOTANICAL NAME: *Lactuca sativa*

The most definitive work on salads is John Evelyn's *Aceteria: A Discourse of Sallets*, published in London in 1699. A country gentleman, Evelyn was well versed in gardening. *Aceteria* lists an astonishing number of plants—forty-eight of them to be exact—that are suitable for *sallet* (what salad was called in the past). Today, an extensive range of salad greens are grown worldwide; more than 800 types are available in the United States alone.

Easy to grow, lettuce likes cool weather. Plant at least two or three different seasonal

---

How to Make a
SALAD

Cut lettuces into small pieces so that they're easier to mix in a salad bowl. Add a little endive (most varieties have pleasant and mildly bitter leaves) and radicchio for additional flavor and crunchiness. Watercress, which has delightful sharp-tasting leaves, and slightly bitter arugula are delicious together or by themselves. My favorite is the tangy, flavorful mesclun, one of the most popular salad greens served at top French restaurants. Don't forget to add edible flowers, such as nasturtiums. This attractive addition will dress up any salad.

---

greens together. Try 'Little Gem', which is one of the best-tasting and most trouble-free summer lettuces you can grow, or the soft green-leafed 'Bibb'. Also, select a leafy type such as 'Buttercrunch'. Lettuce seedlings should be surrounded by sawdust to protect them from snails and slugs (see page 91).

ONIONS {oignons}

BOTANICAL NAME: *Allium cepa*

The word "onion" comes from the Latin *unio*, which means "single" or "one"—referring to the fact that the onion plant produces a single bulb, unlike its cousin garlic, which produces many small bulbs. Originating in northern Asia and Palestine, the onion has been cultivated for more than 5,000 years. It was highly esteemed by the Egyptians and the Greeks, who attributed great therapeutic qualities to it. The different varieties of onion are distinguished mainly by their color.

Onions should be grown from small plants purchased at the garden center rather than from seeds, which take a very long time to grow.

❧

Early onions, such as scallions, are wonderful in salads.

❧

PEAS {*petis pois*}
BOTANICAL NAME: *Pisum sativum* var. *hortense*

A pea is a small, round green seed. Up to eight peas are enclosed in a long green pod. Peas have been cultivated as a vegetable since ancient times. They did not become widely appreciated in Europe until the seventeenth century, when they became the favorite vegetable of Louis XIV and his court. Peas are rich in phosphorus, potassium, and vitamins A and B.

Peas are generally propagated from seeds sown directly in the ground. They need a rich, moist soil to thrive. Peas are best when picked young and eaten immediately.

POTATOES {*pommes de terre*}
BOTANICAL NAME: *Solanum tuberosum*

Potatoes are a starchy, tuberous vegetable. Originally grown by the Incas, potatoes were discovered in Peru by the Spanish explorer Francisco Pizarro and brought to Europe in 1553.

A perennial, potatoes are grown from tubers (old stock) with a sprout that has emerged. A large garden is needed to grow potatoes in any quantity. My advice is to buy them at the farmers' market.

RADISH {*radis*}
BOTANICAL NAME: *Raphanus sativus*

Part of the cabbage family, the radish is cultivated for its edible root, which is eaten raw, often as an hors d'oeuvre. There are many varieties of radish, which come in different sizes, shapes, and colors. Radishes are rich in mineral salts (sulphur, iron, and iodine) and in vitamin C.

Radishes grow quickly. Plant the seeds in the garden, and after a few weeks you will have a crop of tasty radishes.

❧

I adore fresh, pink radishes served with sea salt.

❧

SPINACH {*épinard*}
BOTANICAL NAME: *Spinacia oleracea*

Originating in Persia, spinach comes in many varieties. In the Middle Ages it was served either fresh or chopped, cooked, and then pressed into balls called *espinoche*. During the seventeenth century in France it was fashionable to cook spinach with sugar. Spinach is rich in minerals, especially iron and vitamins.

Spinach is partial to cool weather and grows quickly.

ZUCCHINI {*courgettes*}
BOTANICAL NAME: *Cucurbita pepo*

The delicate-tasting zucchini is low in calories.

Zucchini is easy to grow in a wide range of soils and climates. Do not forget to mulch around established plants to prevent weed growth. Be sure to water zucchini well.

Fruits

Growing fruits adds to the garden and is very rewarding. Imagine all the jams and preserves that you can make from your crop. Furthermore, the many fruit-bearing shrubs, vines, and bushes require little attention.

BLUEBERRIES {*myrtilles*}
BOTANICAL NAME: *Vaccinium*

Blueberries are easy to grow. They need a cool climate in the winter to be successful in the spring. A strong, acidic, peaty soil that is well drained is also important. To ensure your blueberry bush produces fruit, do not prune it during the first 3 years, because the berries are born on the previous year's wood. For best results, plant blueberry bushes by themselves.

MELONS {*melons*}
BOTANICAL NAME: *Cucumis melo* var. *reticulatus, Citrullus vulgaris* (watermelon)

The melon is believed to have originated in Asia and was known in China at least 1,000 years ago. It was brought from Naples, Italy, to France by Charles VIII (who reigned from 1483 to 1498). There are several melon varieties, among them watermelon, honeydew, and cantaloupe. Jean-Baptiste de La Quintinie, Louis XIV's gardener, cultivated several in the kitchen garden of Versailles. I am partial to the small, orange-fleshed Cavaillon melon.

Melons need to grow in a climate with a long, hot summer and low rainfall—unless they are grown under a glass cloche.

> To prevent the flesh from discoloring, melons should not be cut with a steel knife.

> Melons should be eaten with a fork, because the back of the spoon anesthetizes the taste buds.

RASPBERRIES {*framboises*}
BOTANICAL NAME: *Rubus idaeus*

Raspberries come in many hues—from red, purple, and yellow to black. Low in calories and full of vitamins, calcium, iron, and phosphorus, this delicate fruit is simply delicious.

Since the raspberry bush is not very attractive, don't place it in the middle of your flower garden. It likes a well-drained soil, which can be largely clay or sandy loam. Feed the soil with a strong fertilizer when first planting the bush, and water often. You must be the boss of your raspberry patch or this plant will quickly take over, become diseased, and provide you with nothing but small seedy fruits. Do not forget to cut back the old canes.

RHUBARB {*rhubarbe*}
BOTANICAL NAME: *Rheum rhaponticum*

A hardy perennial, rhubarb originated in northern Asia. One of the first signs of spring, the sight of red knobs poking up when everything else is asleep in the ground fills a gardener with delight. There are many varieties of rhubarb, with stalks ranging from green to shades of mauve. I am partial to 'McDonald' and 'Valentine'. Until the eighteenth century, rhubarb was only regarded as a medicinal and ornamental plant. The English first introduced it to the kitchen. With a calorific value of only sixteen calories per hundred grams, rhubarb is hardly fattening. However, it is fairly sour, and thus sugar is called for in most recipes. Rhubarb is full of vitamins including phosphorus, potassium, magnesium, and iron.

The normal growing season for rhubarb is May to July, but early, forced bright pink rhubarb is delicious and tender. At the end of May or the middle of June (depending upon the weather) the stalks turn tough. If you want to start rhubarb in your garden, grow it from roots planted in autumn or winter (when the plant is dormant). Otherwise, plant in the spring. Always set the crowns two to four inches below soil level. Don't harvest any stalks until after the third year. It is also important to remove the flower stalks as soon as they appear in order to conserve the plant's strength. Unlike with most plants, never cut the stalks; instead, pull them. Avoid feeding rhubarb plants with manure, which will invite disease. If fertilizer is needed, use chemical plant foods. Watch out for snails and slugs, especially when the plants are young. Divide your rhubarb patch every 5 or 6 years by separating the roots.

Like sweet corn, rhubarb's sweetness begins to turn starchy the minute the stalk is pulled from the garden. The produce sold in supermarkets doesn't have the taste of the homegrown variety. Farm stands are a good alternative if you decide not to grow it yourself.

Rhubarb should be used within 2 days of being pulled. Store the stalks in a cool place or they will become soft.

There are a couple of tricks for preparing rhubarb for cooking: Choose tender, medium-size stalks that are thick, crisp, and release sap when snapped. Peel the dry skin from the bottom of the stalks and trim off the leaves. Peel the larger tougher stalks but bear in mind that the color is better if they are left unpeeled.

❧

Rhubarb jam and compote are often flavored with lemon zest or ginger. The compote makes a tasty accompaniment to fish. Rhubarb chutney is equally divine.

❧

Tarte à la Rubarbe
RHUBARB PIE

SERVES 6 TO 8

My grandmother made her irresistible rhubarb pie with chunks of fruit instead of stewed fruit. I am fond of the texture and love the design of the latticework piecrust. Sometimes I make a variation using half apple and a little less sugar.

¼ teaspoon butter for coating the pie pan
15 rhubarb stalks, scrubbed
Two 9-inch store-bought piecrusts (preferably Pillsbury)
1 cup granulated sugar
1 teaspoon sea salt
½ teaspoon grated nutmeg

1. Preheat the oven to 350°F. Butter a 9-inch pie pan, and set aside.

2. Strip off the outside skin of the rhubarb stalks. Cut the stalks into ½-inch pieces and place in a large bowl.

3. Press one piecrust into the base and sides of the pie pan, and trim the excess dough, leaving about a ½-inch overhang. Lay a 1-inch layer of the cut rhubarb on top of the crust.

4. Add sugar, salt, and nutmeg to the remaining rhubarb, and pour into the lined pie pan.

5. Place the second piecrust on a piece of parchment paper. Cut the dough into 1-inch-wide strips. Lay four strips, evenly spaced, over the rhubarb filling. Create a lattice pattern by weaving 3 more strips over and under the bottom strips on a diagonal. Crimp the edges of the dough to create a seal.

6. Bake in the oven for 45 minutes, or until the crust is golden brown. Cool on a wire rack, and serve warm or at room temperature.

STRAWBERRIES {*fraises*}

BOTANICAL NAME: *Fragaria chiloensis × F. virginiana*

Strawberries are a rewarding crop for the home gardener. They grow in most climates and soil types. New plants will continually produce if you replant the runners that develop after flowering. It is important to keep your strawberry patch clear of weeds, which can suffocate the plants. Also, protect strawberries from slugs and snails (see Other Ways to Combat Bugs and Insects on page 91).

Delicate *fraises des bois* (wild strawberries) are deliciously fragrant.

TOMATOES {*tomates*}

BOTANICAL NAME: *Lycopersicon esculentum*

There are many varieties of this fruit—from heirloom and yellow to cherry. In France and Italy, the tomato has been nicknamed the "golden apple" (*pomodoro*). Tomatoes are low in calories and rich in vitamins A, B, and C.

Warm growing conditions are essential for tomatoes to flourish. If planted against a sheltered wall that receives full sun, tomatoes will ripen within the growing season. One way to create a warm shelter is with bales of hay, which will absorb and distribute the heat. In order to produce clean, ripe fruits that do not take up too much room, tie the plants to stakes. Select a stout pole, about four feet long, and hammer it about one foot into the ground, approximately six inches from the tomato plant. Using soft twine, tie the stems to the stake as the plant grows. Be sure to carefully remove the suckers that grow out from the leaves near the stem, without damaging the flower stalks or main stem. This will ensure the growing fruit receives plenty of sunlight.

Planting and Tending a Fruit Orchard

Fruit trees have glorious blossoms and look good year round if well cared for. So consider growing fruit trees instead of ornamental varieties; it is much more satisfying. One of the prerequisites to getting a good crop is a sunny spot. Make sure that your fruit trees have plenty of space. Do not put large-growing fruit trees too close together. They will soon overlap and prevent sunlight from reaching the fruits. Choose a warm and sheltered spot with protection against the wind for the best results. Even a small city backyard has space for a citrus tree or two. These trees will produce a good yield over several months. Remember that for many fruit trees, such as apples or pears, you may need a male and a female specimen for cross-pollination.

❧

To protect fruit trees, tie cardboard around their trunks in late summer. This will lure moths, grubs, and weevils. Remove the cardboard after a week or two and destroy it.

To ensure an abundant crop, cover your trees with netting to prevent the birds from eating your fruit. Place some aluminum foil on the tree's branches; the reflection will scare away the birds.

❧

APPLES {*pommes*}
BOTANICAL NAME: *Malus pumila*
Apples are the most widely cultivated fruit in the world. They originated in Asia Minor and were growing wild in Europe by prehistoric times. Unlike dinosaurs, they have survived, much to our enjoyment. For those of us trying to fight the battle of the bulge, bear in mind that an apple is only 52 calories per 100 grams.

Apples are also popular because they grow in a wide range of soils and climates with a minimum of maintenance required. Choose at least one from among the following varieties: 'Red Delicious' or 'Golden Delicious', 'Cortland', or 'Jonathan'. For late apples, choose among 'Baldwin', 'Northern Spy', and 'Rome Beauty'. All are pollinators, which is necessary for fruit production.

❧

For delicious applesauce, I use a combination of several types of apples, such as 'Red Delicious', 'Cortland', 'Jonathan', and 'Granny Smith'. For a flavorful touch, add a little lemon or orange juice, and a few drops of vanilla.

❧

APRICOTS {*abricots*}
BOTANICAL NAME: *Prunus armeniaca*
The apricot tree grew wild in China 1,000 years ago. It was later grown in India and then in Persia and Armenia, from where it gets its Latin name. Greeks call the apricot the "golden egg of the sun." Apricots are rich in carotene, vitamin A, magnesium, calcium, iron, sodium, and fluorine. This fruit is delicious eaten fresh from the tree.

Apricots do best in climates with warm summers and cool winters, and not much rain during the spring and summer seasons.

CHERRIES {*cerises*}
BOTANICAL NAME: *Prunus avium*
Cherry trees are spectacular in the spring, when their delicate blossoms appear. Keep in mind that you need a male and a female for pollination. Relatively easy trees to grow, they do best in climates with a cool winter and warm spring. Good soil conditions are also important. Do not prune cherry trees in winter.

FIGS {*figues*}

BOTANICAL NAME: *Ficus carica*

This ancient plant is mentioned in both the Bible and the Koran. Figs contain beneficial minerals and vitamins for digestion. They have more fiber than other dried or fresh fruits.

Growing figs is not difficult. With its sculptural leaves and great smell, this tree can double as an attractive potted plant.

GRAPEFRUIT {*pamplemousse*}

BOTANICAL NAME: *Citrus × paradisi*

The grapefruit tree needs to grow in a warm climate, because it is sensitive to cold. Like all citrus, it requires fertile soil with good drainage.

LEMONS {*citrons*}

BOTANICAL NAME: *Citrus limon*

The lemon tree was appreciated by both the ancient Greeks and Romans. A beautiful ceramic tile depicting the fruit was found in the ruins of Pompeii, and a mosaic tile discovered in the ruins of a Roman villa in Carthage, North Africa, shows a lemon growing on a branch.

Growing a lemon tree can be a rewarding experience. Requiring little space, lemon trees only produce fruit in a mild climate (Zones 9 through 11). Once the tree blossoms, it can take from 4 to 12 months for fruit to appear. During this flowering period, the tree relies on insects for cross-pollination and fruit development. Highly sensitive to cold, lemon trees should be planted near the south side of the property, and they need protection from frost. They also require full sunlight for adequate growth. While lemon trees can tolerate a range of soils, a well-drained, slightly acidic one is preferable.

Tarte aux Figues Très Facile
THE EASIEST FIG TART

SERVES 6 TO 8

This flavorful fig tart is simple to prepare. Make sure to select figs that are ripe and firm, and purchase a good-quality apricot jam.

¼ teaspoon unsalted butter
One 9-inch store-bought tart pastry
1 dozen fresh ripe figs
1 teaspoon rum
One 4-ounce jar of apricot jam
Whipped cream (preferably homemade)

———

1. Preheat the oven to 350°F. Butter a 9-inch tart pan with a removable bottom, and set aside.

2. Roll out the pastry until it is about ¼ inch thick. Line the tart pan with the pastry, centering it in the pan. Press the dough evenly into the bottom and sides. Crimp the edges at the top of the pan. Prick the bottom of the pastry with a fork, and dot with butter.

3. Bake the pastry until golden brown. Remove from the oven, and cool on a wire rack.

4. Peel the figs, making sure to discard the stem. Cut the fruits in half crosswise, and set aside.

5. In a medium bowl, mix the rum with the apricot jam. Run the mixture through a sieve. Then spread most of it over the pre-baked tart shell, reserving a little for coating the fig slices.

6. Overlap the fig slices on top of the jam-coated tart shell. Coat them with slightly melted apricot jam. Cut the tart into wedges and serve. For extra drama, top with whipped cream.

Lemon trees make great houseplants. They are comfortable in containers as long there is adequate drainage and room for growth. Heights of around 3 to 5 feet tall can be expected. A good soil and frequent feedings of a citrus fertilizer, such as Miracle-Gro, will result in a hardy tree.

NECTARINES {brugnons}

BOTANICAL NAME: *Prunus persica* var. *nectarina*

The history of the nectarine runs parallel to that of the peach, which appears to have originated in China about 2,000 years ago. Nectarines, in essence, are peaches that lack a fuzzy skin; instead they have a smooth one. As with peaches, nectarines have a juicy flesh and can be white or yellow; on average they are slightly smaller and sweeter than peaches.

Nectarine trees, just like apple trees, must be grown in regions with a cool winter to allow the tree to lie dormant for a period of time. In natural settings, the trees live for around 40 years, some reaching 30 feet in height. In orchards, the trees are kept at around 12 feet tall to make harvesting easier.

ORANGES {oranges}

BOTANICAL NAME: *Citrus* × *sinensis*

Originating in China and mentioned in ancient texts, this citrus fruit was considered a luxury before the eighteenth century. The sweet orange appeared in Europe in the late 1400s, the era of Christopher Columbus. After trade routes were closed in 1453, when the Turks defeated the Byzantine Empire, centered in Constantinople (Istanbul), many European kings began to seek alternate trade routes. Sea routes opened trade with China and India. With the introduction of the sweet orange tree to Europe, the dynamics of the citrus fruit's importance throughout the world changed. The voyage of Portuguese explorer Vasco da Gama recorded that in 1498 there were multitudes of sweet-tasting orange trees in India. The new sweet orange variety, known as the "Portugal" orange, caused a dramatic surge in citrus planting. During the early nineteenth century, California developed a hardy and juicy species, known as the "Washington" navel orange.

❧

Oranges are very rich in vitamins, particularly vitamin C.

Oranges grow best in climates that have warm to hot summers and mild winters. Rich soil with good drainage is essential. You can also plant these attractive trees in pots.

❧

PEACHES {*pêches*}

BOTANICAL NAME: *Persicum malum*

The peach tree originated in China where it has been known since the fifth century BCE. It was introduced to Japan, and then to Persia, where it was discovered by Alexander the Great. Its name comes from the Latin, and means "Persian apple." Under Louis XIV, many varieties were grown at Versailles by Jean-Baptiste de La Quintinie. The fruit was nicknamed "*le teton de Venus*" (the breast of Venus), signifying how much it was loved. Peaches are rich in potassium and vitamins A, B, and C, and are good for the digestion.

The ideal climate for peaches is a warm to hot summer followed by a cool winter. Peach trees need good drainage, but they can thrive in many different kinds of soil provided they get lots of sun. With a lifespan of about 12 years, typical peach cultivars begin bearing fruit in their third year. Peach trees are prone to a disease called leaf curl, which usually does not directly affect the fruit, but does reduce the crop yield by partially defoliating the tree. The fruit is very susceptible to brown rot (or dark reddish spots). To prevent it, monitor the tree in the spring for blossom infection and prune out any cankers and infected shoots.

PEARS {*poires*}

BOTANICAL NAME: *Pyrus communis*

Pears were beloved by the ancients. Homer called this fruit a "gift of the gods." Roman horticulturists used grafting techniques to develop more than fifty different pear cultivars. Hardy varieties of pears spread throughout Europe and Britain as Roman conquerors carried pear seeds on their conquests, while Asian orchardists developed their own pears. In the nineteenth century pears flourished throughout Europe. France was known for producing the best dessert pears, and many varieties were brought to England after the Norman Conquest in 1066. Today there are more than 3,000 known types grown around the world. Certain heirloom varieties are high on my list of favorites: There's 'Bartlett', an early ripening pear with a sturdy shelf life, which is delicious in salads or eaten out of hand; 'Anjou', both red and green, with its luscious white flesh that gets even sweeter a few weeks off the tree; the crisp 'Bosc', which holds up beautifully when poached in red wine or baked in a buttery pear tart; the petite 'Seckel' (also known as the Sugar Pear), which is spicy and aromatic—a wonderful choice for a blue cheese, walnut, and frisée salad; and 'Comice', with its succulent sweetness and custardy texture, perfect for a simple dessert. Pears, depending on the type and region, are in season from early spring to late summer. Pears are one of the few fruits that improve off the tree.

Pear trees have the same basic growing requirements as apple trees: a winter that is cool to cold, a spring with low rainfall, and a warm summer. Pear trees live a long time, from 50 to 75 years, and can reach a considerable size if not carefully trained and pruned. Within 4 to 7 years of settling in, the tree will start to bear fruit. Note that they take several years to mature, and do not produce a heavy crop until 7 years from planting.

PLUMS {*prunes*}

BOTANICAL NAME: *Prunus domestica*

Plums are mentioned in writings dating back to 479 BCE, including Confucius's list of the popular foods of China. Plum trees were cultivated in Syria and grafted by the Romans, who preserved them by drying them. From the sixteenth century on, plums were widely cultivated. The plum is a juicy but fairly acid fruit

with a high sugar content containing potassium, calcium, and vitamins. Many varieties of plum, in yellow, green, red, and purple hues, are popular; among them, 'Reine Claude', 'Catherine', 'Imperiale', 'Czar' (in England), 'Mirabelle', and 'Quetsche'.

The different plum varieties each require specific climate and soil conditions.

Companion Planting

Companion planting, a centuries-old technique, is a great way to combat pests and diseases. This inexpensive natural planting method is not only safe for the environment but also extremely effective.

Bear in mind that raspberry and blueberry bushes should not be planted in close proximity because their soil needs and growing habits are very different. Each time I have planted blueberries near raspberries, my blueberries have ended up not bearing fruit, or worse, even dying.

- Plant basil with tomatoes.
- Plant chive with carrots.
- Plant dill and mint with cabbage. (Avoid growing dill near carrots.)
- Grow garlic near raspberries.
- Grow horseradish near potatoes.
- Since lemongrass attracts bees, it is beneficial to include it in a garden with fruit trees. The pollinating bees will help with fruit-bearing trees and make vegetables thrive.
- Plant nasturtium with cabbage and radishes.
- Plant rosemary with cabbage, beans, and carrots.

A water source for the garden is essential—this old-fashioned cistern catches and stores rainwater.

Keeping Pests Away

My children think that our kitchen garden is rabbits', woodchucks', and other animals' supermarket, and in some respect it is. But you can prevent this from being so by building a sturdy fence around your garden. Three feet is tall enough; make sure that it also extends 3 inches into the ground and is fastened to stout posts. You also need to keep insects and bugs from harming your plants.

However, encourage wildlife, such as birds and frogs, into your garden. They will feast on slugs. And, some bugs, like ladybugs, are good for the garden because they eat aphids.

My Trusty
ANTI-GREEN FLY POTION

1. Fill a bucket with 1 gallon of water.

2. Add 3 tablespoons of liquid soap and 2 crushed garlic cloves to the water.

3. Fill a spray bottle with the solution and spray it regularly on your trees and bushes.

USING HERBS, VEGETABLES, AND FLOWERS TO COMBAT BUGS AND INSECTS

Basil repels flies and mosquitoes.

———

Strongly aromatic, **chives** exude a scent that repels insects.

———

Garlic makes an excellent insect repellent.

———

Horseradish repels potato bugs.

———

The **African marigold** is a wonderful green pest deterrent. Easy to grow from seed, this hardy plant will thrive almost everywhere. Once established it doesn't need much attention. I like to give my marigolds a sprinkling of warm tea once in a while, and if the weather gets very hot I water them. Their roots, stems, and petals emit a chemical that insects find unpleasant. Toss a few petals around your garden.

Nasturtiums lure aphids away from fruits and vegetables, and also repel the white fly. Plant nasturtiums near the vegetable garden as they will attract green flies from the surrounding area, keeping them away from your precious vegetables.

———

To help your trees grow, put 2 gallons of small whole **potatoes** around their roots.

———

Boil **rhubarb** leaves in water, and then dilute the mixture and spray it onto plants to repel aphids and caterpillars.

———

Due to its fragrant foliage, **rosemary** can be made into an insect-repelling spray.

OTHER WAYS TO COMBAT BUGS AND INSECTS

Add **coffee grounds** to your garden. High in nitrogen, they increase the soil's acidity, and a wide range of pesky creatures can't stand them. Both slugs and cats are coffee haters. The grounds will also sometimes serve as an effective olfactory-based repellent for picky deer.

Catnip (*Nepeta cataria* L.) is an excellent plant for your garden as it repels mosquitoes, houseflies, cockroaches, and termites. It doubles as an ingredient for tea, known to reduce stress and promote good sleep.

Deer are not fond of really strong smells such as bars of **scented soap** or cheap perfume. A neighbor of mine has kept her beautiful hosta beds free of deer for years by placing Irish Spring soap on stakes throughout the garden.

To get rid of Japanese beetles, which eat foliage and flowers, drop them in a metal can with a little **kerosene** in the bottom. Garlic also repels them.

Make humane slug and snail traps by burying bowls of **beer** in the soil. The odor of the beer will lure these bugs, which creep into the liquid, get drunk, and drown.

Another green slug repellent are the half-rinds from **citrus fruits** such as grapefruit and oranges. Strew them throughout your garden, and the slugs will flock to them. Come morning, throw the rinds in the trash or throw them onto your compost pile to dry out in the sun.

A narrow line of **sawdust** or holly leaves around the garden bed will also deter snails.

To prevent snails and slugs from climbing up potted plant containers to eat their contents, apply a thick layer of **petroleum jelly** around the pot, about 1 inch from the top. This method can also be used around the holes in tree bark.

Place a collar of **heavy paper** around the stems of newly planted tomatoes to prevent worms from nibbling them.

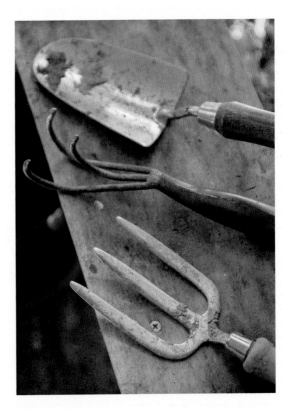

Chapter Three

SPRUCING
UP

Embracing the simple pleasures of a well-kept home will increase your happiness. Making the effort to tidy up and clean your surroundings will reward you with a positive outlook on life, and make you house-proud.

Over centuries the French have developed a distinctive savoir faire for better living, which is achieved through several classic methods of sprucing up the house. These methods have been handed down from generation to generation. They are as relevant today as in the past. Our grandparents knew how to maintain a home by implementing simple natural recipes. For me, the smells of lemon, savon de Marseille, and lavender evoke wonderful childhood memories. These three ingredients were beloved by my grandmother, who believed that they can clean and "improve" anything, provided you know how and when to use them. Let me share with you these treasured secrets.

CLEANING

Cleaning is a highly therapeutic process that produces instant gratification. When objects are in place, dust is under control, kitchen cabinets are organized, the bathroom is sparkling clean, and the bed is made, life seems instantly better. There is something magical about being seated in a clean room—the crisp aroma of newly washed laundry freshening the air like a summer breeze. You will suddenly feel in control of your life. Do not wait for spring-cleaning. Start now.

For me, the following basic products are essential to clean, maintain, and make all the nooks and crannies of a house smell and feel wonderful: baking soda, Borax, lavender, lemon, salt, savon de Marseille, and white vinegar. My ancestors understood the incredible benefits of all of them.

Basic Cleaning Products

BAKING SODA

A miracle of nature, most baking soda is made from trona ore, mined from natural deposits throughout the world. Baking soda is a combination of carbonic acid and sodium hydroxide. It is best known for baking—as a rising agent when mixed with cream of tartar.

BORAX

An extremely effective antibacterial, fungicidal, cleaning, and bleaching agent, Borax is an environmentally safe product that has low toxicity.

LAVENDER

Lavender has been considered a miracle plant by French grandmothers for generations because it has such an array of health benefits and culinary uses. The oil extracted from its leaves helps to heal burns, cuts, and stings, while its flowers deter flies and moths. Lavender is also believed to reduce anxiety, depression, and headaches, and its lovely scent encourages sleep. This multipurpose plant also comes in handy in the kitchen—it is a gentle flavoring agent used in cooking and baking.

LEMON

The cleaning and antiseptic qualities of lemon have been appreciated for centuries. Lemon is also an essential cooking and baking ingredient.

SALT

Salt is a household cleaning staple that also is used in cooking and has health benefits.

SAVON DE MARSEILLE

Only a few savonneries near Marseille still make this legendary soap in the traditional manner. Known for its purity and use in gentle skin care, savon de Marseille's smell is heavenly. It takes a soap master two weeks to make savon de Marseille. The delicate mixture of olive oil, alkaline ash from sea plants, and sea salt is heated for ten days in antique cauldrons, and then poured into open pits where it hardens. Cut into large cubes and stamped, the bars of soap are then set out to dry in the sun. This versatile product, when rubbed on door hinges, will prevent them from creaking; if a drawer sticks, rub some on its edges.

WHITE VINEGAR

For 10,000 years this fermented alcohol has had hundreds of different uses. The Babylonians discovered its preserving properties. The Romans drank it. The Greeks pickled vegetables in it, and sailors used it to treat scurvy. White vinegar is a versatile liquid that has multiple uses—from cooking, killing weeds, and healing wounds to cleaning glass and melting away grease. When you combine vinegar with baking soda, you've created "cleaning gold." Stock several gallons in your kitchen.

My Equipment Care Tips

Before using a new broom with natural bristles, soak it in a sturdy bucket filled with a mixture of 2 cups warm water and 3 tablespoons of table salt for 30 minutes. This will toughen the broom's bristles and it will last longer.

Soak dishcloths in a solution of baking soda and warm water for 10 minutes to freshen them. Afterward, rinse well with cold water, and air-dry.

Wearing rubber gloves will not only protect your skin, it will also allow you to use hotter water, ensuring cleaner dishes.

Change the batteries in your smoke and carbon monoxide detectors twice a year.

MY GRANDMOTHER'S GO-TO CLEANING SOLUTION

(Lemon and White Vinegar Solution)

This homemade solution—my grandmother's miracle cleaning product—features white vinegar and lemons as its main ingredients. Use it to clean a number of surfaces, including mirrors, glass, countertops, and floors throughout the house. The pleasant smell will bring a smile to your face.

1. Fill a thoroughly cleaned 8-ounce glass jar with the peel from 1 lemon. (You can use any citrus fruit you like, but I prefer lemon.) Pour enough white vinegar to fill the jar, and screw on the lid.

2. Let the mixture sit for two weeks, and then remove the lemon peel.

3. Mix the remaining liquid with equal parts water and vinegar, about ¼ cup each, or less.

4. Use the solution to clean surfaces in the kitchen and throughout the rest of the house.

❧❧

Other useful homemade cleaning solutions—from mists to pastes and other products—are provided throughout this chapter.

❧❧

ESSENTIAL CLEANING SUPPLIES

- Vacuum cleaner and a supply of vacuum bags
- Iron and ironing board
- Mop
- Bucket
- Sponges (a variety of types with and without abrasive surfaces)
- Broom and dustpan
- Dusters (feather, microfiber cloths, and other types)
- Spray bottles
- Plunger
- Rubber gloves
- Dishcloths
- Paper towels
- Brushes, including scrub, nail, tooth, and toilet bowl
- Rags and cloths, including wool (made from cut-up old sweaters), cotton (made from cut-up old sheets or T-shirts), terry cloth (made from cut-up old bath towels), chamois, flannel, all lint-free

NECESSARY SAFETY EQUIPMENT

- Extra smoke and carbon monoxide detectors
- Fire extinguisher

KITCHEN CLEANING AND UPKEEP

WHEN HOUSEKEEPING, FOCUS on one room at a time, starting with the kitchen. Here are a handful of practical, easy-to-follow tips that have been vetted by generations of French families.

Kitchen Appliances

DISHWASHER

The dishwasher collects gook and can smell bad. On top of that, the dishes that have been washed in it might not be as sanitary as they should be. Every six months remove the dishwasher filter and soak it in warm soapy water for about 10 minutes. Put the filter back in place, and then pour 1 cup of white vinegar on the bottom of the dishwasher. Turn the dishwasher on the heavy cleaning cycle. When the cycle is completed, sprinkle baking soda on the bottom of the dishwasher. Leave overnight, and then do a second heavy cleaning cycle. When it is finished, your dishwasher will smell like new again.

To remove hard-water deposits, run the faucet until the water is hot, and then begin the dishwasher cycle. After a few minutes, stop the dishwasher. Add a package of Tang (or citrus Kool-Aid) to the detergent bin. If you have one of the larger 20-ounce containers of Tang, add the rest of the powder to the bottom of the dishwasher. Now run a full cycle and the citrusy goodness of the powdered drink mix will eat away any hard-water deposits.

DRAINS

To deodorize drains, pour 1 cup white vinegar down the drain, leave for ½ hour, and then flush with running cold water. When a sink drain is clogged, pour 2 tablespoons baking soda down the sink immediately followed by ½ cup white vinegar. Let sit for about 20 minutes (the solution will bubble), and then flush with cold water.

GARBAGE RECEPTACLES

Garbage Can

To remove unpleasant odors, sprinkle baking soda into the bottom of the can. Add 1 cup water and swirl it around. Pour the water out and leave the can to dry. Then add 3 tablespoons baking soda for the next time.

Garbage Disposal

Many people love garbage disposals because they make it easy to get rid of food scraps, saving countless trips to the outdoor trash bin. Unfortunately, they also tend to get stinky with prolonged use.

MICROWAVE

To clean and deodorize a microwave oven, fill a microwaveable bowl with vinegar and boil it in the microwave. This will loosen dried food on all surfaces, which can then be wiped clean with a soft cloth.

OVEN

Know your oven's cleaning capabilities. For a self-cleaning oven, set aside the time to let it run through its cleaning cycle. First remove the racks. Soak the racks for several hours in warm, soapy water (be sure to use a dishwashing liquid that has grease-cutting properties) and then scour, rinse, and dry them.

If you do not have a self-cleaning oven, scrape off any major spills with a stiff plastic spatula. Add 3 tablespoons of baking soda to a spray bottle, fill with warm water, and shake to thoroughly mix. Spritz the inside surfaces of your oven. Let them sit for 10 minutes and then wipe them down with a paper towel.

Wipe spills as soon as they occur. For stubborn stains, sprinkle salt over them while the oven is still warm (wear an oven mitt to protect your skin from burning). Wipe the surfaces clean after the oven has cooled down.

REFRIGERATOR

Thoroughly clean the refrigerator on a weekly basis. Dump rotten food or produce, expired yogurt, and condiments you bought three years ago and never had occasion to use, in the trash.

❧

My Tips for Cleaning the Refrigerator

Take out the shelves and drawers and wash them in the sink to make sure you don't miss any hard-to-reach spots. Don't forget to wipe down the interior walls of the refrigerator. Dissolve 1 tablespoon Borax in 4 cups warm water. This mixture will clean and deodorize at the same time.

To eliminate smells and sticky spills, create a paste of water and baking soda. Apply it with a rag to remove most of the stickiness. This paste helps to neutralize basic odors and leaves a relatively subtle scent behind.

❧

STOVETOP

Gas range burner grates are an ordeal to clean. Oil and grease buildup on the metal solidifies after numerous heat cycles, reaching a point where it can be difficult to remove. So, every night wipe down the grates with a cotton rag to alleviate buildup.

How to Clean

STOVE BURNER GRATES

1. Remove the grates from the stovetop, and clean them with a cotton cloth dipped in white vinegar.

2. If the grates are very dirty, put them in resealable freezer bags. (The bags need to be large enough to hold the grates and still be closed completely.)

3. Carefully pour 1 cup white vinegar into each bag. Seal the bags, and let them sit overnight (outdoors if possible).

4. Take the grates out of the bags and wipe them down with a sponge.

5. Dry the grates with a hair dryer as you should never cook on a wet grate.

Kitchen Equipment

BASKETS

Baskets, with their simple and sophisticated designs, have always been a staple in the French pantry. They come in all shapes and sizes—oval to round with a handle—and are usually made from cane, rush, willow, or raffia. They can be used for picnics, or to hold, carry, present, and display fruits, cheeses, vegetables, breads, and even silverware on the table.

My Tips for Cleaning Baskets

Dust baskets with a duster (not one with feathers) twice a year.

Hose them down with warm water once a year during the warm weather so that they can air-dry outside.

CUTTING BOARDS

In my grandmother's day, a good old-fashioned wooden cutting board was used in food preparation. Today, wooden cutting boards are still preferable to plastic, glass, or ceramic, because they don't dull your knife blades. It is important to keep boards for bread and vegetables separate from those used for meat.

My Method for
CLEANING WOODEN CUTTING BOARDS

Do not put a wooden cutting board in the dishwasher. Instead, hand wash as follows.

1. Wash the surface with warm, soapy water.

2. Fill a spray bottle with two parts white vinegar and one part freshly squeezed lemon juice diluted with a little water. This solution will disinfect and deodorize the wood. Shake the bottle, and then mist the board.

3. Follow with a final scrub and then rinse.

FOOD COVERS

I love old-fashioned glass food covers. They are good for protecting and displaying a wide range of foods that don't need refrigeration—from chocolate and cakes to cookies and dry fruits.

Covers for Refrigerated Food

An upturned dinner plate works well for covering leftover food that needs cooling down prior to refrigeration. Wrap perishable food in plastic wrap, tin foil, or wax paper. Or, place it in a plastic, glass, or metal container.

My Method for
CLEANING GLASS COVERS

---

1. Wash the covers in warm, soapy water or liquid dishwashing detergent, and then rinse with warm water. If the glass is particularly dirty, add a drop or two of white vinegar to the soapy water.

2. Dry with a dishtowel.

3. For extra sparkle, fill a small plastic container with water and a few drops of white vinegar. Dip a sponge in the solution and rub each glass cover. Rinse under the faucet, and then dry with a clean, lint-free cloth (linen is ideal). Otherwise, water spots will remain on the glass.

GLASS

My grandmother's cupboard was filled with crystal glasses, which were brought out on special occasions. Today, it is fashionable to mix crystal with everyday glassware (see page 210).

My Method for
CLEANING CRYSTAL

---

1. Wash each piece in warm soapy water in the sink. Rinse them well with warm water mixed with 1 teaspoon white vinegar.

2. Let the crystal dry upside down on a dishtowel to avoid water stains.

FOR DIFFICULT STAINS

1. Rub each piece with a lint-free cotton cloth soaked in rubbing alcohol, and then follow the directions above.

My Method for
MAKING A VASE SPARKLE

1. To remove residue, clean the vase in a bucket full of warm white vinegar mixed with 1 teaspoon table salt.

2. Rinse the vase in warm water.

3. Rub the surface with a thin slice or two of raw potato, and rinse again in warm water.

4. Dry with a lint-free cotton towel.

My Method for
CLEANING A DECANTER

1. To clean the hard-to-reach inside, make a solution of 2 tablespoons baking soda, the crushed, dried shell of 1 egg, and ¼ cup warm water.

2. Swirl the liquid around the inside, and let sit overnight. Pour out the liquid, and rinse with a mixture of water and 1 teaspoon white vinegar.

3. Rinse well under the faucet, and air-dry, upside down on a dishtowel.

KNIVES

Knife care is incredibly simple and intuitive, and yet nobody seems to follow the "rules of the blade." No matter how much your knives cost, you'll need to do due diligence to keep them sharp. Remember that a sharp blade cuts best, and also is safer. Dull knives are more difficult to use. Applying pressure to tough foods can cause the knife to slip and harm you.

My Tips for Knife Care

Keep knives dry. This will ensure better edges. The blades are made from thin, delicate steel, which rusts quickly when exposed to water and air. Even true stainless-steel knives aren't really stainless; their chromium coating only slows down the advance of rust and corrosion. Never leave a steel knife soaking in water. Wipe the knife down with a slightly damp sponge, rinse it off, dry it with a dishtowel, and immediately return it to where you store it.

Knives belong in one place. A knife block is ideal since it keeps the knives from bumping into other utensils.

Depending on how much you use them, knives should be sharpened at least twice a year. Either bring them to a local sharpening service or sharpen them yourself using a steel for European-style knives and a Japanese waterstone for Japanese knives.

BATHROOMS SHOULD BE kept clean and orderly for hygienic, practical, and aesthetic reasons. Organize toothbrushes, combs, lotions, and other essentials in an attractive manner. Powder rooms should be guest ready. Make sure to have nice soap bars or pump soaps and clean towels.

Porcelain Sinks, Toilets, and Bathtubs

My Tips for Keeping Porcelain Shiny

Fill a small plastic takeout container with two parts water to one part white vinegar. Dip a lint-free cloth or sponge into the solution and rub the surface.

To get rid of mineral deposits, rub the surface with the freshly squeezed juice of one lemon (diluted with 1 cup water) and rinse well.

FAUCETS

To get rid of lime deposits on faucets, soak a rag in white vinegar, wrap it around the faucet and any other areas where there is buildup, and let it sit for about 1 hour. Then, clean the faucet with warm water.

SHOWER CURTAIN

To rid a shower curtain of mildew, mix 1 tablespoon table salt with the freshly squeezed juice of two lemons. Rub the stains with a sponge dipped in the mixture. Let the curtain dry, and then rinse with water.

SHOWERHEADS

If the showerhead is clogged with lime buildup or other mineral deposits, remove and soak it in a large metal bowl or basin filled with 1 cup white vinegar and 3 cups water (or, one part vinegar to three parts water). Let the showerhead sit in the solution overnight, and then rinse it clean in cold water.

THE TOILET BOWL

To keep a toilet pristine, clean it at least once a week. Fill a spray bottle with two parts white vinegar and one part water. Spray inside the bowl, brush with a toilet brush, and flush. Repeat if any stains have not been successfully removed, and re-flush.

BATHROOM TILES

To rid bathroom tiles of mildew, spray or wipe tiles with a solution of four parts water to one part white vinegar. Let the solution set for 1 hour, and then remove with a clean sponge or paper towel. Sprinkle some baking soda on a toothbrush, and scrub the grout lines clean.

SURFACES AND MATERIALS

A HOME IS a reflection of a person's life—rooms become filled with objects and furniture that have been collected, bought, or inherited through the years. Patina adds character and charm. It is important to maintain and properly care for collectibles and fine surfaces. Here are my cleaning methods and tips.

Alabaster to Silver

ALABASTER

Alabaster looks like marble and is used to create vases, statues, lamp bases, and other ornamental objects. Fine-grained but soft enough to be scratched with a fingernail, alabaster can be easily broken, soiled, and weathered and so must be handled with care.

❧

Dust alabaster frequently with a soft terry-cloth rag.

Do not use water on alabaster as it can stain it. Instead, clean with Borax, which will not scratch the surface. Dip a moistened cloth into a small amount of dry Borax, and rub the object. Buff dry with a soft rag.

❧

BRASS

Try this cleaning method for restoring the shine to brass.

> *My Method for*
> ### CLEANING BRASS
>
> 1. Make a paste of equal parts flour, table salt, and white vinegar in a small plastic takeout container.
>
> 2. Using a cotton cloth, apply the paste generously to the surface of each piece. Let it sit for 15 to 20 minutes.
>
> 3. Remove the paste residue with a damp cotton cloth. Then rub with a second clean damp cotton cloth until the surface shines.

BRONZE

Try this cleaning method for removing the tarnish from bronze.

My Method for
CLEANING BRONZE

1. Pour 1 teaspoon freshly squeezed lemon juice onto a soft cloth and rub each piece.

2. Rinse the piece with warm water. Dry with a soft dry cloth.

FOR DIFFICULT STAINS

1. Brush the stains with a toothbrush dipped in a mixture of ⅓ cup white vinegar and 1 tablespoon table salt.

2. Rinse with warm water. Dry the piece with a soft cotton cloth and buff until shiny.

My Tip for Cleaning Gilt Bronze

—

If the piece is extremely tarnished, brush it with a cloth dipped in warm red wine. Rinse with ¼ cup ammonia mixed with 1 cup water.

CHROME

This cleaning method for chrome will bring back its luster.

My Method for
CLEANING CHROME

1. Make a paste of baking soda and water (see Marble on page 111). Apply with a terry-cloth rag to the piece's surface.

2. Rinse well with warm water to remove all deposits. Buff with a terry-cloth rag.

Never leave salt on chrome as it will corrode the surface.

COPPER

Try this cleaning method for restoring the shine to an old copper pot without getting your hands dirty.

My Method for
RESTORING COPPER SHINE

—

1. Boil 3 cups white vinegar with 1 tablespoon table salt in a large metal pot.

2. Submerge the copper pot in the solution for 3 to 4 hours.

3. Remove the pot, and then dry and buff the surface with a wool cloth.

This second method is also quite effective but requires dirtying your hands.

RESTORING COPPER SHINE
Alternative Method

—

1. Mix together 1 cup white vinegar and 1 cup freshly squeezed lemon juice in a small porcelain bowl.

2. Clean the copper with a toothbrush dipped in this solution.

3. Rinse each piece under the faucet.

4. Dry and buff each piece with a soft cloth to avoid scratching the surface.

To make the outside of a copper pot or pan stay shiny longer, apply a little bit of clear beeswax to a thoroughly clean surface. Let dry and polish.

LEATHER

Leather must be maintained and cleaned regularly to keep pieces and surfaces from looking dull.

My Method for
LEATHER STAIN REMOVAL

---

1. Sprinkle my favorite green cleaning product Terre de Sommières, which can be purchased online, on the stain.

2. Let the wet stain dry overnight.

3. Buff the stained area with a soft cloth.

If your leather furniture and objects look dull, rub them with the inside of a banana peel. It will immediately bring back the leather's original brilliance.

If a small leather surface has become dull, rub it with the inside of an orange peel. This method works well to restore brilliance.

If a leather piece is getting old and starting to crack (or your cat has scratched it), rub the surface with a cloth dunked in warm whole milk. Let the piece dry for several hours and then polish it with a wool cloth.

MARBLE

Baking soda, a light abrasive and a natural disinfectant, is tough on stains and germs. Admire how it brings back the sparkle of marble.

MARBLE CLEANING PASTE

---

1. Make a thick paste using approximately ¼ cup baking soda and 3 tablespoons water in a small plastic takeout container. Alternatively, use toothpaste (but not gel-based).

2. Apply the paste generously to the stained area. Let sit for about 1 hour.

3. Scrub the surface gently with a new scrub brush or a clean terry-cloth rag.

4. Wash off the paste with a fresh, wet terry-cloth rag. Repeat if necessary.

SILVER PIECES

Clean silver pieces often to avoid tarnish. Your silver will retain its shine much longer. I use my grandmother's old-fashioned way of cleaning silver when I have the time (see below). Today, with time constraints, it may be easier to turn to a silver dip to restore tarnished silver. Simply dip pieces into it, rinse them in warm water, and then buff them with a soft chamois cloth.

My Method for
THOROUGHLY CLEANING SILVER PIECES

1. To clean severely piqued silver, heat 2 cups white vinegar in a medium-size pot.

2. Place the silver pieces in the pot and add enough water to submerge them. Let the silver soak in the vinegar/water mixture for at least ½ hour.

3. Rinse the pieces in warm water, dry with a soft cotton cloth, and polish with a chamois or wool cloth.

My Method for
CLEANING SMALL SILVER OBJECTS

1. Place objects in an aluminum pot filled with water and 2 tablespoons table salt.

2. Bring the salted water to a boil. In a short time you should see results without getting your fingers dirty.

3. Dry with a soft cotton cloth to avoid scratching.

MY GRANDMOTHER'S SILVER CLEANING TECHNIQUE

1. Add 1 teaspoon ammonia to a sink filled with warm, soapy water.

2. Soak the silver pieces for 10 minutes.

3. Wash each piece quickly under the faucet, using a very soft brush.

4. Rinse each piece in clean hot water.

5. Dry each piece with a linen towel, and then rub with a chamois cloth.

Wood: Furniture to Floors

Before wood can be used for creating furniture and floor beams (or, for building a house), it must be seasoned to stabilize it and to prevent shrinkage and warping. However, wood remains sensitive to moisture. It may expand and warp in damp conditions or shrink and split if the air is very dry. For this reason, consider having a humidifier—especially if you own valuable antiques or have central heating.

Wood falls into two categories. Hardwoods come from broad-leaved trees, such as oak, mahogany, ash, walnut, elm, maple, cherry, and teak. Softwoods come from trees with needle-like leaves, such as pine, spruce, redwood, and cedar. Softwood is generally lighter than hardwood and is often painted, stained, or veneered. The more exotic woods, such as satinwood and ebony, are used primarily for veneer.

Following are my favorite methods for cleaning and stain removal. It is extremely important to test a small area of any surface before proceeding. For seriously damaged (or precious) pieces that need special treatment, such as for wood burns, turn to a professional.

My Go-To Methods for CLEANING AND BRIGHTENING WOOD SURFACES

1. Mix 2 tablespoons olive or boiled linseed oil, 1 tablespoon white vinegar, and ½ tablespoon turpentine in a metal bowl.

2. With a lint-free cotton cloth dipped in this solution, rub the surfaces about twice a year.

3. Polish the surfaces immediately with a dry piece of flannel.

REMOVAL OF GLASS RINGS FROM POLISHED WOOD

1. In a bowl, mix together 2 tablespoons vinegar and 2 tablespoons vegetable oil.

2. Dab a soft rag into the solution and then rub the wood, along the grain, to make the ring disappear.

Charming wood samples (from top to bottom)—oak, chestnut, and acacia—with painted French inscriptions and leaves.

SPECIAL WOOD SURFACES

GILT WOOD

For this old-fashioned French technique dating from the eighteenth century for cleaning gilt wood, do not use a towel, which might chip the gilding. Instead, use a feather duster to remove dust buildup. For a more thorough cleaning, carefully apply one egg white, beaten in a metal bowl, to the surface with a paintbrush. Let the egg white air-dry, and then lightly run a silk cloth across the surface of the wood.

MAHOGANY

Warm white vinegar takes out most stains. Pour a little vinegar on a lint-free wool cloth and rub the surface gently.

POLISHED WOOD

Rub surfaces with a sponge dipped in beer at room temperature. Then dry quickly with a soft towel.

VARNISHED WOOD

Mix equal parts (about 1 cup each) olive oil and turpentine in an old glass, metal, or porcelain bowl. Rub the mixture slowly on the wood until it shines. This technique will also help to remove watermarks.

WHITE-WASHED FURNITURE AND PICKLED WOOD FLOORS

The old-fashioned French way to clean white wood surfaces is with the cooking water from boiled potatoes. Reserve the cooking water in a large glass container. Pour a little of it on a terry-cloth rag and rub the furniture and floor surfaces. Make sure not to soak the wood.

FLOOR CARE

NICE CLEAN FLOORS throughout the house make a difference. Floors are the fifth wall. Nothing is better than the smell of a freshly polished floor. This smell brings back memories of happy times spent at my grandmother's house.

MY GRANDMOTHER'S HOMEMADE FLOOR POLISH

1. Cut 4 ounces beeswax into small pieces.

2. Pound a piece of resin the size of a walnut with a knife. Melt the beeswax and resin together in a pan on the stove.

3. Let the mixture cool and stir in 1 quart turpentine.

4. Rub a little bit of the mixture on the floor with a piece of flannel, and then polish with a dry flannel and soft brush.

MOPPING WOOD FLOORS

1. Fill a bucket with cold water and add a squirt of dishwasher detergent.

2. Dunk your mop in the soapy water and go to it. Start in one corner of the room, planning your exit strategy so that you don't mop yourself into a corner. (For polyurethane-coated hardwood floors, run your mop along the wood grain.)

3. Once your mop starts to look dirty, wring it out. Replace the soapy water with clean water and repeat the mopping process. When finished, dump the dirty water down the toilet instead of in the sink. Let the floor dry before walking on it.

Note: Avoid mopping waxed hardwood floors as water may cause damage.

My Tips for Wood Floors

Sweep floors regularly to remove any dust or dirt, which can scratch the surface.

If grease spills on a wooden kitchen floor, pour cold water on it immediately. The water will harden the grease and prevent it from soaking into the floor. Carefully scrape up the mess with a knife.

My Tips for Tile Floors

A green option for cleaning tile is using the cooking water from boiled potatoes (see how to clean Pickled Wood Floors on page 115).

Use cotton rags for washing tiled floors (rags should also be used for brick or slate floors).

To clean off black marks made by shoes, use a rag to rub a little bit of water mixed with ammonia across the tiles.

RUGS AND CARPETS

THE FLOORS OF most homes are covered with either area rugs or wall-to-wall carpets that need a good cleaning on a regular basis. If you want your rugs and carpets to last, you must care for them properly.

Brooms and sweepers are a gentle way to clean a rug or carpet. Vacuuming often to get rid of dust and dirt is more effective. However, extra care must be taken when vacuuming. High-powered vacuums (such as the bagless Dyson or Oreck) will pull threads out of the backs of rugs and carpets and cause loose fibers, or "sprouts." Instead, use the handheld attachment on rugs and carpets. Note that the vacuum's beater bar will pull fibers from rugs and carpets and can cause fuzzing. To avoid fuzzing, turn the vacuum's beater off or put it on the highest setting. Or, use a canister-style vacuum without a beater bar. To do a thorough cleaning, you should rent a steam cleaner or send the rug to a rug specialist.

Rugs placed in direct sunlight will fade over time. Make sure to rotate them every 3 to 6 months, depending on the amount of foot traffic. Wool rugs will eventually shed. Hand-knotted rugs shed less than tufted rugs. Sprouts, which are common to handmade rugs, can be clipped with scissors. Creases in new rugs should disappear within a week or so. If they don't, try reverse-rolling the rug.

RUG CARE TIPS

❧ If a rug is encrusted with lots of dirt and/or is very dusty, either vacuum it or, even better, clean it outside. Hang it on a strong clothesline, sufficiently high enough that you're able to use an old-fashioned beater, and whack out the dirt. Always do the beating from the back, and never beat the pile as doing so will drive the dirt back into the knots. Note that hooked or knotted rugs should never be beaten, because the knots will get caught.

❧ Running the vacuum over a rug's edges will cause deterioration and loosen the fibers around them. To avoid destroying fibers, carefully place the vacuum on the edge of the rug. Also, fringes on the ends of rugs can be destroyed by vacuuming.

❧ To remove wet red-wine stains from a rug, blot the area with a cloth. Soak a clean sponge with carpet cleaner or soda water and blot the stain. Repeat if necessary.

❧ For heavy soil removal from antique rugs, turn to a professional. Dyes can bleed and some rugs are fragile and so can unravel.

❧ To deodorize rugs, sprinkle baking soda on the dirt spots. Leave for 1 hour and then vacuum. This method also works well for dog and cat "accidents."

Rugs that have been stored in a plastic bag may have a musty odor. If the smell doesn't dissipate in about a week, sprinkle baking soda on the rug. Leave for 1 hour and then vacuum.

Do not use water to clean a sisal or natural fiber rug or carpet.

My Go-To Old-Fashioned Method for Freshening Carpets

Sprinkle the carpet with damp tea leaves (Earl Grey or green tea are ideal). After about 2 hours, sweep off the leaves, and then vacuum.

Use a sponge soaked with liquid soap and warm water for grease and dirt removal. First test a small area. Rub the wet spots dry with a clean cloth.

Removing Heavy Soil from
CARPETS

Bear in mind that thorough cleaning requires a steam cleaner, which you can rent, and is labor intensive. Alternatively, turn to a professional.

1. Mix together ¼ cup table salt, ¼ cup Borax, and ¼ cup white vinegar in a small plastic takeout container. Combine the mixture into a paste.

2. Vacuum the area a few times to get rid of dust and dirt.

3. Apply the paste to the heavily soiled areas of the carpet with a rag. Test a small area first to make sure that the paste doesn't leave a mark. Leave the paste on the carpet overnight.

4. Once the paste has dried completely, vacuum the carpet again. Then steam clean the entire carpet.

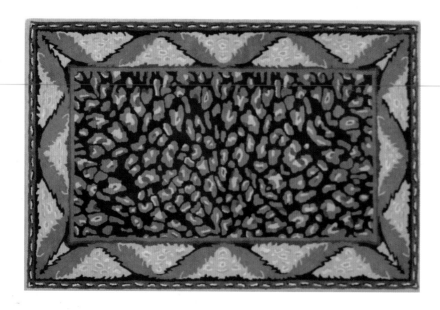

A whimsical painted floor that resembles a carpet design.

MY GO-TO GENERAL HOUSEHOLD TIPS

DUSTING

There are many kinds of dusters. Feather dusters are popular because they do a good job of removing dust from tight spaces. However, they may not be the best choice for allergy sufferers. Microfiber cloths are a great alternative, because they grab and hold a ton of dust without releasing it into the air. Specialized dusters include ostrich-feather dusters, which are ideal for small fragile objects, and lamb's-wool dusters, which are great for flat surfaces.

To dust high (or hard-to-reach) spaces, wrap an old rag around the end of a broom.

Light bulbs need to be cleaned at least four times a year. For kitchen bulbs, on which grease can accumulate, remove the dust with a cloth lightly dipped in rubbing alcohol.

Lampshades need to be dusted on a regular basis. Use a duster for paper or fabric lampshades. For fabric lampshades, use a hairdryer set on cool to blow off the dust, followed by a cloth. For parchment lampshades, clean the dust carefully with a microfiber cloth.

To prevent parchment lampshades from drying out, rub them with a little bit of clear beeswax every six months.

ODOR REMOVAL

Creating a fresh-smelling house is important. Following are my go-to ways to eliminate unpleasant odors, such as cigarette smoke and pungent food smells:

TIPS FOR ELIMINATING UNWANTED ODORS

- When cooking onions, cabbage, or fish, place a pot filled with 1 cup white vinegar on the stove and let it boil.

- To remove stale odors in cookie tins or lunch boxes, place a piece of bread dipped in white vinegar into the container and leave it overnight. In the morning the smell will be gone.

- To eliminate the smell of cigarette smoke, leave a saucer filled with 2 teaspoons of white vinegar in the room overnight.

- Some common spots are gym bags, hampers, and the refrigerator. Set an open box of baking soda inside the refrigerator, or sprinkle a little on top of washable items.

- Keep half a lemon or lemon slices near the sink in a cup. Use them to clean your nails after peeling vegetables, and to deodorize your skin.

WASHING AWAY SPOTS FROM PAINTED WALLS

Save the tea leaves from tea served at breakfast or teatime. When you have accumulated a sizable quantity (about 3 teapot's worth), steep—not boil—them for ½ hour in a metal pan. Strain and use the tea liquid to wash painted surfaces. It will remove spots and give a fresher, newer appearance than soap and water would.

WASHING WINDOWS

Cleaning dirty glass windows takes time and elbow grease. If you use the right method and tools, this chore will go more quickly. Here are my two go-to methods.

CLEANING WINDOWS

1. Brush the window frames and sills to remove any dirt.

2. Dissolve a little liquid soap in a bucket or dishpan of warm water.

3. Dip an old flannel cloth into the water.

4. Start cleaning the window pane at the upper corner by dragging the cloth carefully straight down, making sure that the liquid does not run onto the window sash. Then clean the next line until you've reached the other side of the window. To avoid streaks, wring out the cloth after each stroke.

5. Polish each pane with a chamois cloth.

CLEANING WINDOWS
Alternative Method

1. Make a solution of ½ part vinegar and ½ part warm water in a small bowl.

2. Pour the solution into a spray bottle.

3. Spritz the glass panes.

4. Rub each pane dry with a soft cloth, moving from the top to straight down.

5. For a great shine, polish the panes with crumpled newspaper.

THE FIREPLACE

Thoroughly clean the bricks inside your fireplace during the warm weather, when the fireplace is not in use. From start to finish, the cleanup will take roughly 1 hour depending on the fireplace size. Use a wet sponge sprinkled with table salt to scrub the bricks, and then wipe them with a wet cloth. If the bricks are a natural color, apply a light coat of natural beeswax afterward, and polish the surface with a wool cloth. The wax will protect the bricks and give them a lovely patina.

Place white birch logs in the fireplace during the months of the year when you don't light fires.

Using the Fireplace

Have at the ready dry split logs in a large basket or other attractive container by the fireplace. If you live outside the city, keep a surplus of wood neatly stacked outside (or in the garage), protected from the elements. Buy wax-dipped pine cones, which will create bursts of color when thrown into the fire. If your fire is weak, toss in a handful of table salt. This will revive the flames.

For an aromatic twist on a cold evening, toss in orange or lemon peels, and some cinnamon. Old potpourri will also make for a wonderful smelling fire.

Keep a fire extinguisher handy. Make sure that everyone in your family knows where it is and how to operate it. In addition, baking soda can also be used to scatter over the flames. Baking soda will also help to quell the flames from electrical and grease fires.

THE LINEN CLOSET

A WELL-ORGANIZED LINEN closet is not only a pleasure to behold, it is also a way to make your life run much more smoothly. If you have the space, store your bed, bath, and table linens separately.

Table Linens

Tablecloths and napkins, along with good sheets, are the ultimate luxuries for your home. A table covered with a tablecloth will immediately say that today is special and my guests are worth it.

Tablecloths and napkins are an elegant component for entertaining. In literature Honoré de Balzac mentions the state, quality, and whiteness of the table linens when describing a meal. And, indeed, the whiteness of a tablecloth is among the first, indispensable signs of elegance. Its length is another. Having a tablecloth falling in large folds around the table legs was considered the height of luxury during the eighteenth century. Today, you can cover your table with a freshly ironed tablecloth of any color or pattern. A simple brunch, or lunch, will be elevated with the addition of linen napkins or crisp, neatly folded tea towels (see Napkins and Tablecloths on page 212).

Tablecloths should be stored together with their napkins, neatly folded and tied with ribbons. This orderly system will save you time when setting the table.

MY WASHING TIPS

Contrary to what is often said, no amount of salt or white wine will remove red wine spilled on a white cloth. You need to flood the stain with cold water immediately, and then spray lots of Shout on it. Hot water will set the stain and only make it harder to remove. As soon as the stain dries, you will have more difficulty getting rid of it. For small stains, non-oily eye-makeup remover is very effective as are baby wipes. Test a small area first.

My Method for
BRIGHTENING A WHITE TABLECLOTH

This method also works for a white T-shirt.

1. Add 1 teaspoon of cream of tartar to a quart of boiling water in a stockpot.

2. Soak the item in the water for 30 minutes.

3. Wash the item in the washing machine.

FOR DIFFICULT STAINS

1. Add a couple of shavings of savon de Marseille and a slice of lemon to the boiling water.

2. Follow Steps 2 and 3 but soak the item for an additional 30 minutes.

Add ¼ cup white vinegar to whites during your washing machine's final rinse cycle to help remove soapy residue. White vinegar also softens fabrics and reduces static.

Traditionally, in the French countryside, cooks put dried or fresh thyme into the water used for washing linen tablecloths to add a lovely scent.

If you do not have gentle laundry detergent, use baby shampoo.

Beds, Bed Linens, and Blankets

A bedroom is the sanctuary where we relax and rejuvenate. Making it as inviting as possible will provide joy and a comforting atmosphere. Maintaining and keeping beds, bed linens, and blankets pristine is important.

How to Fold a
FITTED SHEET

1. Hold the sheet vertically, one corner with each hand, and fold it in half by bringing the corners together with the rounded, elasticized seam on the inside.

2. Repeat from the opposite direction (bottom to top) so that all four corners are joined together and the sheet is folded in quarters.

3. Lay the sheet flat and fold into thirds: Start by moving the rounded-edge side into the middle, and then layer the other side on top.

4. Flip over and stack with matching flat sheets and cases.

TIPS FOR BED CARE

- To keep your mattress in good shape and to prevent sagging, flip it over each season and rotate it twice a year.

- Organize sheets by size. Place the different-size sheets on their own shelves, and label the piles. If you have inherited or collected beautiful sheets and pillows, tie them with old ribbons. This is the old-fashioned French way.

- For heirloom or other special sheets, place a piece of white tissue paper between them or put them in a plastic, zippered bag for protection.

- To give your sheets a fresh, pleasant scent, slip a sachet of dried lavender (see page 134), a bar of fragrant soap, or savon de Marseille into the bag.

- Place pillows in neat stacks and tie (or arrange) them together. These beribboned piles are visually appealing.

- Store clean wool and cotton blankets in zippered plastic bags with a bar of savon de Marseille inside. The soap will keep them smelling fresh as well as bug free.

- Nothing feels better than sleeping on fresh-smelling, ironed linen sheets, the ultimate luxury for me. Sheets washed or ironed with scented water, such as lavender or roses, will make you sleep better. You can also place some dried lavender or roses between the stacks of stored linens.

- To wash wool or cotton blankets, add 2 cups white vinegar to the rinse cycle. This will make them soft, fluffy, and soap free.

My Tip for Cleaning Mattresses

To remove stains, mix one part baking soda to two parts water in a plastic container. Apply the paste on the stain with a cloth. Let it dry (it takes about an hour) so that it has time to leach the stain, and then brush off the powdery substance. Baking soda will also deodorize the mattress.

SWEET WATER
for Rinsing and Scenting Linen

1. Place a mix of aromatic leaves and/or flowers (such as lavender or roses) with 2 cups water in a covered pan.

2. Boil, strain well, and use as a final rinse for hand-washed linens or in the final rinse cycle of your washing machine.

HERB SWEET WATER
Sprinkled on sheets
(and clothing) before ironing.

1. Fill a saucepan with 5 cups water.

2. Add 5 sprigs rosemary, cover, and bring to a boil.

3. Let sit for 1 hour, and then strain well.

4. Add ½ teaspoon powdered orris root to the liquid to fix the scent.

Variation
FLOWER SWEET WATER

Substitute the 5 sprigs of rosemary with 5 fresh lavender flowers and stems. Then follow the directions above.

- Dry sheets, and even clothes, outside on a clothesline, and they will smell fresh (be aware that many neighborhoods have banned this old-fashioned practice). Run a laundry line from north to south for the most sunshine. And be sure it's not near a bird's nest or your items will get dirty very fast. The next best option is to keep a permanent line strung across the laundry room or a spare room.

- Make sure your iron is clean. To get rid of adhesion, rub an emery paper across the flat metal surface.

- Iron only clean items.

- Spritz stubborn wrinkles with distilled water before ironing.

- When ironing a sheet, iron it flat with no creases.

- When ironing a tablecloth, fold it in half and iron in the folds.

- When ironing a napkin, fold it in half and iron in the folds.

(see page 64). The unique spicy scent of lavender is also ideal throughout the home.

The name "lavender" comes from the Latin *lavare*, which means "to wash." Traditionally, it was used in bathwater and laundry water. In warm climates such as the South of France, where the sun draws the fragrance of the flowers into the air, women often drape their laundry over lavender bushes to dry it. The scent is heavenly.

Place bundles of dried lavender in your linen closet among the napkins, tablecloths, sheets, and pillowcases.

Tuck lavender sachets in dresser drawers or under bed pillows.

Lay sprigs of lavender, thyme, or rosemary among sheets and towels. These herbs will protect your linens from moths.

Keeping the Linen Closet Pest Free

If you keep table and bed linens clean and regularly washed, you should have no problems with bug infestation. However, the one herb that works miracles when it comes to keeping the closet pest free is lavender. Its flowers deter flies and moths. Lavender also has other benefits, such as strong antibacterial properties

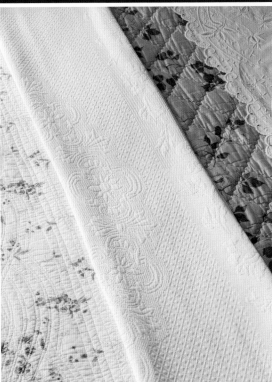

A WELL-ORGANIZED WARDROBE

IT IS IMPORTANT for one's mental well-being to clean out excess items on a regular basis. A well-organized wardrobe reduces stress. Welcome the warm weather by packing up those winter garments the correct way. And, of course, with spring comes balmy weather, which means a change of wardrobe. If you don't have the closet space to handle everything year-round, here are my tips for making your seasonal clothing swap much more manageable.

Edit your belongings. Get rid of old, stretched-out, or unflattering garments. With everything laid out in front of you at the end of the season, you can easily identify the items that you don't wear anymore. Or, ask a friend for her opinion. Instead of throwing out articles of clothing, donate pieces that are still in good shape to a local homeless shelter or Goodwill. For the craft oriented, consider repurposing some old favorites.

Ideally equip closets with matching hangers. There are hangers for different weights of clothing, including silk-covered hangers for delicates.

Mothballs are stinky relics of the past. They smell bad, contain pesticides, and are a little toxic. Instead, place lavender bags (see Lavender Bags on page 134) or blocks of cedar in your closet.

Place nearly empty bottles of a favorite cologne in your lingerie drawer to give your clothes a lovely fragrance.

Store out-of-season sweaters in clear plastic zippered bags and put a bar of savon de Marseille inside each to keep your garments smelling fresh.

Pamper your wardrobe with beautiful hangers and spray them with your favorite cologne.

Wash and clean everything before storing it. I can't stress this enough. Unseen bits of food can attract bugs, and subtle spills that you might miss can set and become harder to remove next season. As if stains aren't horrifying enough, insect eggs that would normally come out through regular cleaning can hatch if they're locked away for six months. Wash everything in water that is as hot as the fabric type will allow. Avoid fabric softener and starch since the emulsifiers can attract beetles and moths. Make sure to thoroughly dry articles of clothing to avoid mold. Take everything else to the dry cleaner.

DRAWER LINING PAPER

Another simple luxury is to line your drawers with pretty scented papers. The textured back of wallpaper absorbs scent well and is ideal. Lay thin muslin bags of aromatic herbs (lavender is the best) between layers of lining paper. Roll the bags and wallpaper up together and wrap the cylinder in plastic wrap for six weeks. Then cut the wallpaper to fit the drawers.

LAVENDER BAGS

It is customary in France to place these small, beautifully scented bags in closets. Lavender bags (also called sachets) are easy to assemble. They also make lovely gifts.

1. Cut small squares from muslin or other fabric remnants.

2. Place a pile of dried lavender in the center of each square and gather the fabric together.

3. Tie the top with a pretty ribbon.

4. Put the bags in the pockets of clothing stored in the closet.

Variation
ROSEMARY OR THYME BAGS

Follow the directions for making lavender bags but replace the dried lavender with either dried or fresh rosemary or thyme.

Clothing Care

Make sure that your clothing is in good shape. If a button is missing, replace it. If you cannot find an identical one, change all the buttons. If your clothing has a hole, mend or patch it.

KNITS

Knit items are very delicate, and so as with jeans, you should keep them away from the washer and dryer (for the most part). If your knits are looking grungy, it's time for a wash. Yarn is similar to human hair, so strong soaps and detergents can damage its fibers. The knitting experts suggest using a gentle shampoo and even conditioner for hand washing your knitted items.

Carefully place knit gloves or scarves in lukewarm water mixed with a small amount of gentle shampoo and conditioner. Press them down slightly until fully saturated, and then let them rest for about a minute. To rinse, drain the sink and fill it with lukewarm water. Add a few drops of white vinegar to the rinse, which will help protect the fibers. Place your knit goods in the washing machine—yes, you read that correctly—on the spin cycle for 10 seconds. This will get rid of excess water without actually wringing it out, which causes knits to lose their form. Do not let your garments spin longer than 10 seconds, or you will end up with misshapen scarves and gloves. To complete the drying process, lay your knits flat on a drying rack or some towels.

WOOL ACCESSORIES

Wool is a textile fiber from any number of animals, including sheep, rabbits, and goats. Each kind of wool must be cleaned differently.

As a general rule of thumb, do not put wool, mohair, or cashmere into the dryer. It is also imperative that you never wring them out.

Sheep Wool

Also known simply as "wool," sheep wool is the most common type of wool. Cleaning this material is a delicate process. Hot water, dryers, and hang drying not only will distort the shape of your garment, they will also ruin the wool itself. Fill a container or sink with warm (not too hot) water and add 1 teaspoon of mild detergent. Soak garments in this mixture for 5 minutes and then press them to make sure they're saturated. Rinse with cool water and lay flat on a few towels to dry.

Mohair

This type of wool comes from the Angora goat, which has soft, silky hair. A mohair item, such as a scarf or sweater, can be cleaned in a similar way to sheep wool. Fill up a sink or basin with lukewarm water. Add a small amount of mild detergent, such as Woolite. Dunk the mohair item and lightly swish the water. Gently squeeze the liquid from the item, and then rinse it with more lukewarm water. Lay it flat on some towels to dry.

Cashmere

Cashmere comes from the undercoat of the Cashmere goat. Clean it the same way you would clean mohair (see Mohair for instructions).

SILK SCARVES

A silk scarf is difficult to clean, and so proceed carefully. The main factors to consider when washing silk are how easily the delicate fabric can pull, and whether or not the dyes will bleed. You should use either a gentle non-alkaline soap or baby shampoo. First, test to see if the soap will discolor the silk by placing a drop or two on a less noticeable section.

Soak the scarf in lukewarm water mixed with a few drops of liquid soap in a basin or the sink. Let it sit for about five minutes, and then rinse it out with cool water. To help keep silk shiny, add some distilled white vinegar to your rinse. Lightly squeeze the scarf to remove excess water and lay it flat on a few towels to dry. If you are feeling adventurous, carefully iron it on a low setting while it is still damp. This ensures a wrinkle-free finish and added shine.

OTHER USEFUL CLOTHING CLEANING TIPS

- Add ½ cup Borax to your washload, along with the usual amount of detergent powder, to boost cleaning power and deodorize the wash.

- Do not wash bras too often (a rule of thumb is to wear them at least four times before washing). To avoid shrinkage, air-dry only.

- Do not wash blue jeans too often. Doing so will shrink them and, in some cases, change the color.

- To freshen baby clothes, add 1 cup white vinegar to the washing machine's detergent dispenser.

- Take care when drying delicate items. Do not hang them, as the weight of the water will distort the shape. Instead, lay them flat on a cotton towel. This also applies to wool and cashmere sweaters.

My Tips for Ironing Clothes

To iron around buttons, carefully work the point of your iron to avoid loosening button threads or damaging buttons. Do not iron over them as they could break.

To iron a dress shirt, start with the collar. Iron from the center out to each point, and repeat on the backside. Then iron the cuffs, the shoulders, and finally the front, back, and sleeves.

MY GO-TO TIPS FOR REMOVING STAINS

STAIN REMOVAL IS a science and an art. It is important to test a small area of fabric or other material before proceeding.

ALCOHOL
Sprinkle the stain with table salt and then pour hot water over it.

BEET JUICE
Drizzle freshly squeezed lemon juice on the stain. Leave for ½ hour. For an old stain, soak the clothing overnight in a mixture of freshly squeezed lemon juice and water, and then wash in the washing machine.

BLOOD
Soak bloodstains immediately in cold water and then wash the garment with detergent in warm water. Sponge a bloodstain on non-washable fabrics with cold water, followed by a small amount of hydrogen peroxide.

CANDLE WAX
Scrape away with a knife as much wax from the article of clothing (or table linen) as possible. Then sandwich the stain between paper towels and press with a warm iron.

CHEWING GUM
Rub the affected area with a piece of ice to harden the gum, and then carefully scrape it off with a dull knife.

ABOVE: I like to use this natural French cleaning product, Terre de Sommières, to get rid of most stains, especially on fabric or leather.

CHOCOLATE
Dab or soak the stain with cold water for 30 minutes. Then rub in liquid detergent and wash the garment with regular laundry detergent.

COSMETICS
Rub the affected area with water and savon de Marseille. Then wash the article of clothing in the washing machine with laundry detergent.

EGG
Scrape off the dried egg with a knife and then sponge the stain with cold water.

FRUIT JUICE

Cover the stain immediately with powdered starch. Let sit for a few hours, and then brush it off and wash the garment.

FRUITS

Sponge the stains immediately with cold water. Do not use soap.

INK

Soak the stain with sour milk. Or, put a little sea salt on it and then squeeze lemon juice on top of that. For an old ink stain, soak the article of clothing in freshly squeezed lemon juice diluted with water. Then rinse in cold water and dry.

METAL

Apply a mixture of $\frac{1}{2}$ white vinegar and $\frac{1}{2}$ freshly squeezed lemon juice with a cloth, and then rinse with cold water.

MILDEW

Mix a solution of freshly squeezed lemon juice and an equal amount of table salt. Rub a generous amount on the stain, and then lay the article of clothing outside, in strong sunlight, on a towel or sheet. Repeat this application, two or three times, until the mildew fades.

PERSPIRATION

To get rid of perspiration stains, rub them with a mixture of one part freshly squeezed lemon juice to one part white vinegar with a cotton cloth. Then rinse and wash the garment in cold water. If this method is not effective, send the article of clothing to the dry cleaner.

RUST

For stains on cotton or linen, squeeze lemon juice on the fabric, and then rub with a towel. Rinse with cold water and repeat. For stains on stronger fabrics (such as wool), make a solution of 4 tablespoons cream of tartar and 4 cups water in a saucepan and bring to a boil. Apply the solution to the stain until the spot is gone, and then rinse the fabric in warm water.

My grandmother taught me these old-fashioned methods. For stains on cotton or colored linen fabrics, place wood sorrel leaves in a juice extractor. Dab the juice from the leaves on the stain and let soak for $\frac{1}{2}$ hour. Rinse with warm water and repeat this process if necessary. For stains on white linen, insert a slice of lemon between two sheets of white tissue paper, and place the stack underneath the stain. Press the linen with a hot iron, making sure not to burn the paper. Rinse the linen with warm water, and repeat this process if necessary.

SOFT DRINKS

Sponge spots immediately with cold water. Then wash in the washing machine.

WINE (red)

Soak the stained fabric immediately in plenty of cold water. If the stain remains, try a stain remover, such as Shout, and soak the fabric in cold water. Do not use hot water as it will set the stain.

OPPOSITE: An old-fashioned *lavoir* used for washing outdoors—a modern washing machine makes this task much easier.

HAIRBRUSH CARE

Soak wood and synthetic hairbrushes with 1 teaspoon of ammonia diluted with warm water. This will prevent the bristles from coming out and also strengthen them.

JEWELRY CARE

To clean gold jewelry (with or without stones), put a dab of regular toothpaste on a Q-tip and rub the surfaces of your item. Rinse in warm water, and repeat until the jewelry is clean. Dry and shine with a wool rag.

LEATHER GLOVE CARE

If your leather gloves cost more than $100, you may want to consider hiring a specialist to clean them. Otherwise, cleaning them at home is a safe (and cheap) alternative. All you need is some saddle soap. Take a dampened paper towel, apply a tiny bit of the soap, and produce a lather. Work the soap into the leather, wipe it away with a damp paper towel, and air-dry.

To clean the grimy insides of your gloves, turn them inside out, and then apply a few drops of Woolite or other gentle detergent. Work the detergent into the leather, and then use a damp washcloth to remove it. If the insides of your gloves still smell unpleasant, spray them with an odor-eliminating product, such as Febreze, then let them air-dry.

SHOE CARE

Shoes for me are very important. I like well-made shoes because they last longer. Following are a few simple guidelines to help keep your shoes pristine.

SHOE CARE TIPS

- Keep shoes clean and polished.

- Use scented shoe pillows to keep shoes in good shape and sweet smelling.

- Repair the soles and heels as soon as they need fixing to avoid permanent damage.

- Fill wet shoes with crumpled newspaper to dry them and retain their shape. Then apply natural polish to the leather.

- To remove bad odors, sprinkle baking soda inside your shoes and let them sit for a couple of hours. Then shake the shoes over a garbage receptacle.

- Spray leather shoes with mink oil to extend their life.

- Spray suede shoes with a water and stain protector (such as Meltonian) to protect them from rain and stains.

NATURAL REMEDIES

THE FOLLOWING NATURAL remedies have been used by French families for generations. They are practical and affordable and don't contain any harmful substances. During my childhood in France, my family often turned to these simple cures. Of course, we went to doctors for serious conditions. Please understand that these remedies may not work for everyone.

BEE STINGS

For relief, rub the sting and area around it with a garlic clove, a sprig of parsley, or a little white vinegar.

BLEMISHES

Take advantage of summer tomatoes and give your face a mask of crushed tomatoes. Cut up and mash one medium-size tomato. With your hands, apply it to your face, making sure to avoid your eyes. Lie down, and leave the mask on for 30 minutes. Then wash your face with warm water and pat your skin dry.

MINOR BURNS AND SUNBURN

For immediate relief from minor burns, place a slice of raw potato on the sensitive area. Also, keep a container of white vinegar in the refrigerator and apply the cool vinegar with a soft cotton pad to relieve pain. To soothe a sunburn, apply white vinegar with a soft cotton pad, or make a sage infusion: Tear a handful of fresh sage leaves and place it in a bowl. Cover the leaves with boiling water, and let the mixture sit for 20 minutes. Then strain it into a plastic squeeze bottle, and apply it to the affected areas. Keep the infusion handy in the refrigerator.

FOOT PAIN

To soothe aching feet, add ½ cup Epsom salts to a large bowl of warm water. Soak your feet for 10 to 30 minutes, or until you experience relief. The salty water will also freshen and soften your skin. When you are finished, rinse your feet in warm water and dry them well.

GAS AND BLOATING

Most herbal teas alleviate gas and bloating (see Herbal Tea on page 147).

HEADACHES

Lie down, and apply a few thin potato slices to your forehead.

HEARTBURN

Sip licorice juice to relieve heartburn. This juice also lowers stomach acid.

INFLAMMATION

Incorporating raw celery and turmeric in your diet may alleviate inflammation. Turmeric is a tasty, peppery spice used in Indian cooking. Mix turmeric in yogurt for a delicious dip.

MOSQUITO BITES

Rub the bite with white vinegar or savon de Marseille to help stop the itchiness and to ease soreness.

SPLINTERS

Soak your finger or foot in a solution of Epsom salts and warm water. The salty water will loosen the skin, enabling easy extraction of the splinter with sanitary tweezers. Then apply a bacterial cream to the wound.

SWOLLEN EYES

If you wake up with red and swollen eyes, apply two warm tea bags (I like Earl Grey, English Breakfast, or green tea) to your eyes. This will take down the swelling. You should also visit your doctor to rule out any eye condition that may require more serious treatment.

TIRED EYES

Make eye pads from thick slices of raw cucumber. Lie down in a comfortable spot, and place the slices on your closed eyes. Relax for a while and you will emerge refreshed.

TIRED SKIN

Boil a handful of fresh chervil (French parsley) in water for about 5 minutes, and then strain the water into a bowl. Once it has cooled, cleanse your skin with the chervil-infused water and a washcloth. This treatment will keep your skin supple.

TOOTHACHES

If you cannot get to the dentist immediately, rinse out your mouth several times with clove-infused water. Boil 2 tablespoons cloves in 2 cups water, and then remove the cloves. Use while warm. Note, the tissue in your mouth is sensitive; you should be extremely careful.

COMMON COLD

Drink this Vitamin Bomb green tea every day to keep colds at bay.

VITAMIN BOMB GREEN TEA

1. Make a pot of green tea.

2. Pour 2 cups of the tea into a blender and blend it with the juice of one orange and 2 tablespoons of ginger, cut up into small pieces.

Lait de Poule
MY GRANDMOTHER'S BEDTIME REMEDY FOR A COLD

Based on experience, I can strongly recommend this recipe.

1 egg
1 teaspoon granulated sugar
A few drops of pure vanilla extract
1½ cups whole milk

1. In a large mixing bowl, break the egg, and then add sugar and scented water or vanilla.

2. Beat with a fork until well mixed, for about 10 minutes.

3. Gradually pour boiling milk into the mixture and keep stirring until combined.

4. Drink the liquid when it has cooled down but is still warm.

The light green bract on the stalk of the linden tree's flower clusters is collected in late spring when the flowers are open, and dried before brewing the tea.

SORE THROAT

An easy and effective remedy is to gargle with salt water.

MARTINE'S LEMON AND THYME-INFUSED WATER

for a Sore Throat or Laryngitis

1 lemon
5 sprigs thyme

1. Boil 4 ¼ cups water in a saucepan.

2. Cut the lemon in half and squeeze the juice in the boiling water.

3. Add one lemon half and let it boil for 3 minutes. Then add the thyme, and boil another 3 minutes.

4. Turn down the heat and let stand for about 30 minutes. Then filter the water. Drink the soothing infused water throughout the day. Add honey for a sweet taste.

PURPLE SAGE INFUSION

for a Sore Throat

1. Make an infusion of 2 ounces fresh sage and 2 cups boiling water.

2. Let steep for at least 15 minutes.

3. Drink half a cup of the infusion four times a day.

4. Gargle with the infusion anytime to relieve throat discomfort.

NOTE: Do not use sage if you are pregnant.

Herbal Tea *(tisane)*

A feeling of warmth and calm. I often yearn for a cup of chamomile, mint, or linden flower herbal tea. Rosehip, lemon verbena, and peppermint teas have the same effect.

CHAMOMILE *(camomille)* is excellent for indigestion, especially an upset stomach and bloating or belly problems. It is soothing and will also help you sleep. When my sleep was disturbed as a child, my mother would have me sip it. The tea lulled me back into slumber.

LINDEN FLOWER *(tilleul)* contains antioxidants and has mucilaginous properties, which can reduce inflammation, soothe coughs and sore throats, and relieve anxiety-related indigestion. This light yellow-green tea has floral notes and is divine when sweetened with honey.

MINT *(menthe)* helps alleviate stomachaches and even chest pains. It is also great for curing head colds by opening clogged nostrils and sinuses. Mint has diuretic properties, too.

HOUSEHOLD PEST CONTROL

UNFORTUNATELY ALL HOUSES at one time or another can be attacked by pests. Natural solutions sometimes work better than stronger chemical ones—besides they are less hazardous to the environment, and also less harmful to children, dogs, and cats. These are some of the tried-and-true methods that have been passed down to me by my grandmother. If there is a real infestation, professional attention is required immediately.

ANTS
A small quantity of green sage placed in the closet will help to make ants disappear. Place the herb on the floor, and then sweep up the dead ants. Slices of lemons are also effective. Another way to catch ants is to put a few almonds on a shelf. The ants will gravitate to the kernels. Brush the kernels into hot water in the sink—you will destroy lots of ants.

BEETLES AND COCKROACHES
Sprinkle Borax on the areas they frequent. A bowl of oranges will also help to keep cockroaches away.

FLIES
To prevent flies from entering your home, plant your window boxes with basil. Small-leaf Greek basil is ideal. Other good fly deterrents are bouquets of mint or peppermint strategically placed around the house. Try also rubbing mint leaves on the woodwork around windows and doors to deter flies.

MICE
Anise seeds make excellent mousetrap bait (cholesterol-conscious mice prefer it to cheese). Mice are also repelled by the smell of mint and tansy leaves, dried lavender, and spearmint and lavender essential oils. Make sure to sprinkle the cellar often with chloride of lime to keep it mouse free. Or, turn to the following preventive method. All work well for cockroach control too.

MICE CONTROL PREVENTATIVE

1. Mix well ¼ pound finely ground cornmeal with ¼ pound plaster of Paris in a plastic takeout container.

2. Add 1 to 2 cups milk, and combine to make a very fine paste.

3. Place the paste in jar lids near mouse hideouts, alongside a small bowl of water.

MOTHS
Cloves stuck into an unpeeled orange is the traditional French way to repel moths. Hang the orange on a doorknob with a string or pretty ribbon. When the orange has shriveled, it is time to throw it out.

Chapter Four

FLOWERS
AND
PLANTS
WITHIN

Flowers, plants, and ornamental trees enliven the home—rooms without them tend to feel empty. For me, they do not just beautify one's surroundings, they also celebrate the seasons and bring nature indoors.

Flowers have been beloved for centuries. The Old Testament mentions how much King Solomon appreciated flowers, crocuses, and lilies in particular. The ancient Greeks liked them, too. The ancient Greek Theophrastus of Eresus even devoted a book, *Enquiry into Plants*, to them, while Virgil sings their praises in many of his poems.

With the discovery of the tulip, the interest in flowers reached its zenith. The tulip, which originated in Persia, was introduced in Vienna in 1554; and in 1601 the botanist Charles de l'Ecluse (also known by his Latin name Carolus Clusius), director of the Royal Medicinal Garden in Vienna, introduced it in Holland. De l'Ecluse had sought religious sanctuary there, and eventually became director of the botanical garden at the University of Leiden. He brought tulip bulbs with him. Both he and his flowers thrived in the Dutch climate, and an incredible industry was born.

Owning tulip bulbs became a sign of wealth. Fortunes were doubled in the blink of an eye. Poor men became rich, and rich men became filthy rich without much effort. In the wildly speculative marketplace of the bulbs, even the threat of government crackdowns didn't halt the illegal trading of the hottest commodity in seventeenth-century Holland. The tulip mania described by the French writer Jean de La Bruyère in his 1688 masterpiece *Les Caractères* swept Europe. The varieties of tulip that sparked this obsession were extraordinarily beautiful. A little shorter than today's hybrids, they had large flower heads with fabulous mottled or "flamed" colors in two-tone mixes of red, oxblood, yellow, purple, and white. Known today as "Rembrandt" tulips, they are featured in many Dutch Old Master paintings.

The notion of having flowers on the table is a relatively modern concept. Until the nineteenth century in Europe, fresh-cut flowers were often considered too rustic for the table and so silk and feathers were used instead. Extravaganzas—including glass bowls filled with goldfish and baby turtles, and elaborate pyramids of fruits piled on cut-glass fruit stands that were sculpted into the shapes of animals or children—made dramatic statements.

By the beginning of the twentieth century these elaborate follies were rejected in favor of lavish floral arrangements. Huge concoctions in oversize

porcelain tureens were the rage before World War I in the grand houses of Europe—from Germany and France to England. The head gardener was in charge of arranging flowers in silver bowls. (Think of the television show *Downton Abbey* and the huge arrangements that Carson places in the great hall.) This was a major production, repeated weekly or even every few days. The flowers were grown in specially planted cutting gardens.

Today the natural look is in for the table, and I love it. Flowers celebrate the earth's beauty, and they should always be fresh and spontaneously arranged, never overworked. They should seem as if they came directly from the garden— even if bought at the supermarket (as mine often are).

PREPARING AND CONDITIONING CUT FLOWERS FOR ARRANGEMENTS

THE FIRST STEP to extending the life of your cut flowers is to condition them before arranging them in a vase or other type of container. Cut flowers are living creatures that need special attention. Handling them with care is essential, and doing so will ultimately save you time and money. Many of my favorite flowers can be kept alive longer if you follow my simple guidelines below.

MY HOMEMADE CONDITIONING LIQUID

Prior to arranging flowers, prepare one of these conditioning liquids. Both work well—it just depends on what you have available.

In a large plastic container, mix together 1 quart lukewarm water, 1 teaspoon granulated sugar, 1 teaspoon bleach, and 2 teaspoons of lemon juice.

— or —

In a large plastic container, mix together 1 quart lukewarm water, 2 teaspoons granulated sugar, and 2 teaspoons white vinegar.

Fresh, clean water and a clean receptacle are critical for cut flowers. Change the water every day. Bear in mind that water evaporates and flowers drink. So fill your container with clean water and make sure to replenish it when the water level goes down.

Cut flowers from a florist or supermarket have probably been conditioned, but it never hurts to recondition them if you have the time. After conditioning, you are ready to arrange them.

Cut multi-headed flowers, such as lilacs or snapdragons, when at least one blossom or cluster is beginning to open and is in full color.

If you have a garden, cut flowers early in the morning, when the stems are fully hydrated, to ensure a long-lasting bouquet. Single-headed flowers, such as sunflowers and dahlias, should be cut when they have bloomed, because they may not open otherwise.

Most flower stems should be cut on a slant, at a 45° angle, to ensure they can absorb plenty of water. Remove leaves and side shoots from the part of the stem that will be submerged in water. This is beneficial in two ways: the water will remain cleaner longer, and the flower will be able to drink through the added openings.

Keep cut flowers in a cool place and out of direct sunlight for as long as possible, and away from heat sources, such as a radiator.

When cut flowers have been properly conditioned and are hydrated, their stems, leaves, and blossoms will be firm. Before arranging, give each stem a fresh cut.

Foliage, even the least delicate, benefits from a short, thorough soaking in lukewarm water prior to being arranged.

Do not keep flowers in your car for any longer than necessary. Even a brief stay in a bitterly cold or brutally hot environment can compromise their resilience, and ultimately their color.

Avoid using especially fragrant flowers, such as hyacinths and lilies, in dining table centerpieces, where their aromas will distract from your meal. Instead, place them in the living room on a side table or a mantel, or in the entryway on a console table.

FOR THE BEST results, each type of flower should be prepared in a slightly different manner. So if you are in a position to invest more time in preparing your flowers beyond general conditioning, the result will be a longer-lasting arrangement. Following is a list of my favorite flowers and guidelines for additional preparation and maintenance.

AGAPANTHUS
This flower will last about a week when placed in water at room temperature with a flower nutrient such as crystal powder.

AMARYLLIS
To extend this glorious flower's life, cut the stem straight across and fill or plug it with floral foam or cotton before arranging. By doing so, you will ensure it lasts as long as it would uncut (see House Plants on page 173).

ANEMONE
To ensure this flower lasts for about a week, place the cut stalk in deep ice water for 15 minutes to make it firm. Anemones will not survive in floral foam.

BABY'S BREATH
Detangle this great "filler" flower by swishing its head in water. Fill a vase with about 3 inches of hot water, a flower nutrient such as crystal powder, and a splash of bleach.

BLOOMING BRANCHES
Clean the bottom of the main branch by scraping off the bark. If it is forked, cut off any smaller branches that might draw water from the main one. Prior to arranging, peel and split the tough stems, about 1 or 2 inches, and then place them in water. If the buds are about to open, the water should be shallow and at room temperature. If the buds are completely open, use a large quantity of cold water. After conditioning, add a flower nutrient such as crystal powder to the water. If possible, leave the branches overnight in the conditioning water in a cool place. The next day, arrange them in a vase or container filled with fresh cool water with some crystal powder added.

CALLA LILY

Cut the hollow stem with a sharp knife and place it in a container filled with cool water and a flower nutrient such as crystal powder. Calla lilies can last up to a week.

CAMELLIA

Keep moist by wrapping the blossom and stem in wet tissue overnight. Note that once cut from the plant, camellias do not absorb water well.

CARNATION

Cut the stem on an angle and place it in a container full of cold water. Before arranging, to accelerate the opening of the blossoms, replace the cold water with warm water. Then add a flower nutrient, such as crystal powder, to the water.

COSMOS

Once the cosmos has been conditioned, arrange them in a vase filled with cold water. Add 1 teaspoon of sugar to the final water to make them last longer. The sugar acts as a stimulant.

DAFFODIL

Once arranged in a vase, add small quantities of cold water to maintain them. Also, add a flower nutrient such as crystal powder.

DAHLIA

To make dahlias last longer, carefully burn the end of each stem with a match after the initial conditioning. Then place them in a bucket with 5 tablespoons alcohol and 3 quarts ice water for at least 30 minutes.

DAISY

Trim daisy stems straight across the bottom. Flip each flower upside down and fill the hollow stem with water. Cover the opening with your thumb, turn the flower right side up, and place it into a bucket filled with room-temperature water. Remove after 2 minutes and arrange in a vase full of water.

DELPHINIUM

Trim straight across the bottom, flip the flower upside down, and fill the hollow stem with water. Cover the opening with your thumb, turn the flower right side up, and place it into a bucket filled with room-temperature water. Remove after 2 minutes and arrange the flowers in a vase full of water.

EVERGREENS

Arranged in a large vase, evergreens make a striking display. I am partial to pine branches, which are also a great filler. After conditioning, place them in a vase filled with 1 tablespoon glycerin and 1 quart cold water.

GARDENIA

After cut from the plant, gardenias do not drink water. Prior to arranging, keep them moist by wrapping the blossoms in wet tissue overnight.

HYDRANGEA

Peel 2 to 3 inches off the stem, split it with a knife, and then dip it in boiling water. Hydrangeas will last up to five days in water. They can also be dried.

How to
DRY HYDRANGEAS

There are many techniques for drying hydrangeas. If done properly, these beautiful flowers will retain their subtle color and last for years. Traditionalists, such as my grandmother, hang them upside down for a couple weeks to dry. However, this is not necessary. My simpler go-to method is as follows: Cut the blossoms from the shrub in late summer, and strip them of their leaves. Arrange in an empty vase and then leave them to dry.

IRIS

After conditioning, fill a vase with a combination of 3 drops peppermint oil and 1 quart cold water.

LILAC

Using a knife, split the bottom inch of the woody stem with a vertical cut. Plunge the stem into a vase filled with cold water and a flower nutrient such as crystal powder.

LILY

Always remove the pollen-covered stamens to make the lilies last longer and also to prevent pollen stains on clothing and tablecloths. Blotting pollen-stained fabric with sticky tape will help with removal.

MIMOSA

The smell of mimosa evokes memories of my childhood—my grandmother's home was always filled with vases of these lovely flowers. Cut mimosas when they are in full bloom. Prior to arranging, remove the lower leaves and place the stems in boiling water. Once arranged, the flower heads benefit from a spraying of cool water. Steam helps, too.

PEONY

Most of us are inclined to reach for the magnificent, fully open pink peony, but hold back. Buy peonies when they're closed. Since they open almost immediately and have a fleeting bloom, you'll want to make the most of them. Trim the stems, place them in a container of hot water to encourage the buds to open, and then replace the water with a pint of cold water mixed with 2 teaspoons of sugar. Remember that peonies wilt quickly in the heat, and so keep them in a cool spot. Make sure to shake or pick off any ants before arranging.

POPPY

Carefully burn the ends of the stems with a match. Place in a container with 2 quarts cool water and a handful of salt. Condition for about 30 minutes prior to arranging.

ROSE

Remove the lower leaves and thorns, and then cut the stems on a slant, under cool running water. This will enable them to drink more water. If you want your roses to open quickly, right before arranging immerse their stems in a container filled with a little hot water for about 5 minutes. Then arrange the roses in a vase, adding one small package of crystal powder or 2 tablespoons salt to 2 quarts of water.

SNAPDRAGON

This flower is available in a variety of cheerful colors, ranging from my favorite strong pink to pale yellow. The medium-height variety is easiest to arrange. Remove the leaves from the bottom of each stalk, and pinch off any dead blooms. Add 2 tablespoons salt to a bucket filled with 2 quarts water. Place the snapdragons in the conditioning water for 30 minutes prior to arranging.

SUNFLOWER

Remove all of the foliage before placing the stems in water. Sunflowers last a long time—at least a week—and may also be dried (follow the drying technique for hydrangeas on page 161).

TUBEROSE

These flowers are long lasting if you remove any foliage below the water line. The florets open along the stem, usually from the bottom up.

TULIP

Remove the lower leaves, and clean off any sand or dirt. Gather together the stems, and roll them in wet newspaper, leaving two inches of stem at the bottom. Give the stems a fresh cut, and then place the bundle in a tall vase full of water for 10 minutes. The tulips will "jump" (spring back to life) as they hydrate. When making a tight arrangement, be sure to re-cut the stems.

ZINNIA

To keep these colorful summer flowers looking their best, push a pin into the stem just under the head and then place the stem in a vase full of cold water.

VASE COLLECTIONS

A BOUQUET OF flowers is an entity, and so the container that holds it plays a decisive role. When you make an arrangement, regardless of its shape, your choice of vase is key. The container will often dictate the form and size of the bouquet as well as the number of flowers needed. Here are some basic rules regarding vases, which I have acquired from years of entertaining as well as those I have learned from my French upbringing.

There is a broad array of vases, in different shapes and materials, to choose from. In my opinion, glass or crystal vases are best as they offer a combination of beauty and practicality. They add sparkle to the table and allow you to see the flowers' attractive stems. Besides you can easily make sure the water level is high enough. If you decide on porcelain, such as blue and white, keep your color scheme simple—all pink, yellow, red, or white flowers. Select colored vases that will complement the flowers in them—a blue vase full of purple blooms or a yellow container of tightly packed orange or red flowers are wonderful combinations. And, bear in mind that odd numbers of vases are more pleasing than even ones. When clustering arrangements, three of each type of vase is ideal.

The great thing about small vases is that they look good from every angle. Groupings of varying heights with a few contrasting flowers make a chic centerpiece. Alternatively, one

small vase with a single open peony or rose and greenery around the base looks lovely on a side table or in a powder room.

Extra-large vases, even filled with expensive flowers, can be overpowering in the wrong setting. However striking a tall centerpiece on a dining table may be upon entering the room, we have all experienced the difficulty of carrying on a conversation with someone half hidden by flowers. Ideally table flowers should fall below eye level. If your bouquet is to be

placed on a mantel or in an entryway where there is plenty of space, this is the occasion to consider a dramatic, oversize vase filled with flowers that have long stems, such as delphiniums or blooming branches.

Unusual containers such as watering cans, *rafraichissoir* (a container similar to a wine cooler), silver timbales, urns, and porcelain pitchers are conversation pieces. An assortment of vintage glass bottles, particularly for

wildflower arrangements, is equally charming. Mix sophisticated peonies in a simple milk jug or place sweet peas in a silver-plated cup.

A vase needs to be watertight. If they are not, put a metal or plastic liner inside. Plastic food containers make great liners. And, always keep your vases perfectly clean. Wash them with soap and water and rinse with a diluted mild bleach solution (despite the strong smell) in between uses.

Flowers should be no more than a third taller
than the vase holding them. Otherwise, they will
be top-heavy and may tip over.

When using a valuable vase on the table,
fill the bottom third with sand to stabilize and
prevent it from tipping over.

For a simple bouquet, use a container
with a smaller neck, which will keep
the arrangement erect.

SIMPLE FLORAL ARRANGEMENTS:
FROM COLOR SELECTION TO COMPOSITION

THINK "EXPLOSION" WHEN making a bouquet. A flower arrangement does not need to be gigantic to be effective. Respect its shape, volume, proportion, and colors. Even the smallest bouquet can project grandeur. When I make a floral composition, I let the colors of the flowers speak to me before I work on shaping them. Always strive for simplicity—it takes a lot of practice to make something look natural.

When making a bouquet, be generous with the number of flowers that you use. It is essential that you gather or purchase more than you think you will need. Also remember that once you strip the leaves from the stalks, you will be left with much less than you started with. Use leftover flowers and foliage to fill up bud vases.

Color

When planning the color scheme for your bouquet, keep the palette simple. Limit the colors and the variety of flowers in the mix to create a more unified and sophisticated look. Bouquets of one kind of flower or one color are the most chic. They are also the easiest to create.

Never design a matchy-matchy arrangement. Flowers that are color-related, or complementary, make for a successful composition. Bear in mind that light flowers say "hello," while dark flowers recede. For me,

the chicest bouquets are limited to one or two kinds of flowers, but sometimes my bouquets have as many as three or four colors.

Composition

A bouquet is like a sculpture. Its structure is integral and is achieved by the organization of the stems. Think of a bird's nest, which is a structural marvel. Its twigs and stems are perfectly intertwined. Turn around the vase and view the bouquet from every angle to make sure that it looks good.

Do not use floral foam to hold up an arrangement. Chicken wire seen through glass or crystal does not look great either, and often it damages the flowers.

Replace the water in your arrangement every day so that bacteria doesn't have the chance to flourish. Be sure to remove leaves that end up below the waterline to prevent rotting.

My trick for making supermarket flowers look great is to cut their stems very short, so short that the flower heads rest on the lip of the vase. Stems should be cut with a sharp knife or scissors, and all leaves that would fall below the water line should be removed. This technique may feel wasteful, but it will have the effect of creating a lovely bouquet out of simple flowers.

When blooms begin to wilt, empty the water from the vase, and cut the stems to create a shorter bouquet. Refill the vase and rearrange the flowers, discarding any that are limp. This is an easy way to extend the life of your flowers.

Do not overcrowd a vase, because it will suffocate your flowers and shorten their lifespan. If you have leftover flowers, place them in bud vases throughout the house.

Cut-Flower Alternatives

If cut flowers are not readily available, there are other creative alternatives. Fresh herbs from the supermarket or your herb garden are a wonderful option. Gather bunches of subtle-smelling herbs and tie them together with raffia to make an unexpected table decoration. Rosemary in silver cups, mint in porcelain pots, or basil in glass jars all look divine. Line up small lavender, geranium, or chrysanthemum plants, transferred to charming pots, down the center of your table. Or, arrange cut branches, with or without blossoms, on its surface. In the spring fill large vases with branches full of pear, cherry, or apple blossoms. In the summer, decorate a table with seashells and lavender or chive blossoms, echoing the seaside landscape. My favorite early autumn displays are rosehips placed in small silver vases and apples set in attractive bowls. For a mid-autumnal look, collect beautiful dried leaves and strew them, along with branches, across your table. During the holiday season, lay pine branches on a silver tray, enhanced with pinecones, either natural or with their tips painted silver or gold. Another easy option is to adorn your dining room surfaces with miniature evergreen trees or rosemary topiaries.

HOUSEPLANTS AND POTTED TREES

HOUSEPLANTS AND POTTED trees give life to a home. For many design professionals, including myself, they are key features. Never before have there been so many varieties of plants and trees available in garden centers. It is easy to find beautiful flowering plants, such as orchids and African violets, as well as topiaries and potted lemon and orange trees.

Throughout history, specimen trees and houseplants have been prized. Charles VIII of France erected the first large greenhouse for orange trees, called an *orangerie*, at his Château d'Amboise, around 1493. In the centuries that followed, the châteaux of the royals and nobility were not complete without their own splendid *orangeries*, each housing an array of specimen trees, houseplants, and flowers.

The fashion for potted trees and exotic indoor plants became an all-consuming undertaking under Louis XIV, the Sun King. The magnificent *orangerie* at Versailles, designed by Jules Hardoin-Mansard, was the culmination. The late seventeenth-century structure took two years to complete. In fact, the plan and construction were finished before the château itself, underscoring how important the *orangerie* was for the king, a fanatical gardener with a special interest in orange trees. He adored their subtle and distinct perfume, which was thought to have aphrodisiac powers. This magnificent square-shaped *orangerie*, which is still extant, is located in the Parterre du Midi at Versailles. More than 1,000 orange and lemon trees, planted in containers (*caissons*), were stored there in the winter, and then wheeled outside in the milder months. Louis XIV used his *orangerie* as an indoor pleasure garden, as well as a place for balls and receptions, for which he decorated the space with myriad rare flowers, plants, and palm trees. Soon *orangeries* had sprung up in all the fashionable spots in Europe.

The *jardin d'hiver* (winter garden) is the child of the *orangerie*. These gardens began to appear in the first half of the nineteenth century. They proliferated during the Second Empire as a result of the huge interest in exotic flowers and rare plants fueled by the universal exhibitions. These "crystal palaces" inspired today's greenhouses and conservatories, which are pleasurable luxuries.

Caring for Houseplants

All indoor plants need special care in order to thrive. Nothing is more important for nurturing their growth than light. Most do best in a southwest window.

Houseplants are divided into two groups: foliage and flowering. Foliage plants are grown for their leaves. Potted in moist soil, they thrive in warm temperatures and diffused light. Flowering plants are plants that produce flowers and fruits as part of their reproductive cycle. Sunlight is needed to produce buds on nearly all flowering plants.

Dust, grease, oil, and other airborne particles can settle on houseplant leaves, making them unattractive and dull looking. Dirty leaves can't absorb as much sunlight as clean ones and thus adversely affect the plant. So clean your plants regularly not only to improve their appearance (we all like to look our best, right?) but also to stimulate their growth and help with insect control. Besides, no plant likes to be left in the corner and forgotten. Plants thrive when you pay attention to them. Follow my advice on general care below.

TEMPERATURE

Plants are like people. Some like it hot, while others like it cold. The best temperature for most plants in winter is 70°F (fluctuating between 45°F and 80°F) during the daytime and 55°F to 60°F at night. There are a few exceptions, such as African violets, which need a very warm environment. A high temperature at night (over 60°F) is not good for houseplants—it will cause leaves to yellow. One reason my grandmother always had success with plants is because the room temperature in her house was lower than what is usual today, especially at night. If you have a chance, put your plants in a cool room, one that is 60°F or lower, at nighttime. You will see how much longer they will live. Signs of too much heat include soft, spindly growth and pale foliage, or if buds drop prematurely.

HUMIDITY

Most contemporary houses are too dry and often too hot for flowering plants. I rely on green-thumb tricks such as increasing moisture by setting a pan of water on a radiator, or placing plants on a zinc tray filled with pebbles on the windowsill. I also resort to my old-fashioned teakettle. It makes plants happy because humidity is released from the boiling water. Plants release moisture, too, and therefore are healthy to have around the house.

WATERING

Watering is an art. Extremes must be avoided. You can do as much damage to plants by overwatering them as you can by under-watering them. Signs of overwatering include brown leaf tips, stunted growth, yellowed foliage, or the shedding of buds. Misting is an excellent preventive. It not only helps to discourage dust from settling and sticking to the leaves, it also keeps the leaves from drying out. Remember to fill your mister with tepid (not cold) tap water. Signs of under-watering include shriveled leaves and dried-out stalks.

A good way to water is to set a potted plant in a large dish, pan, or sink filled with water (the pot should be about half submerged). After the plant is completely hydrated, remove it from the water and allow it to drain. The plant should not sit in water for an extended period of time.

Do not use plastic or glazed pots as they are nonporous and do not breathe. To make such pots more suitable for growing, place a layer of small stones in the bottom to facilitate drainage.

If you repot a plant, water it immediately.

Water plants early in the morning, from top or bottom.

Plants in small pots dry out faster than those in larger pots. Keep a close lookout, particularly on hot days.

Feeding Your Houseplants

Nearly all houseplants will benefit from being fed with organic plant food. Like with any type of fertilizer, however, don't overdo it. Coffee grinds and tea leaves can be used, too.

Mix coffee grounds in the soil of acid-loving plants, such as rhododendrons, azaleas, roses, evergreens, hydrangeas, and camellias. They will add natural acidity and nutrients to the soil. It is better to use the grounds from a drip coffee maker than the boiled grounds from a percolator, because the coffee-maker grounds are richer in nitrogen. There are exceptions—for instance, the acid-loving African violet does not like coffee grounds.

❧

My grandmother used tea leaves (Lapsang souchong and Earl Grey) to nourish her thriving indoor plants. Like me, she drank a lot of piping hot tea. Once it cooled down, any leftover tea was used to water her houseplants. I have followed in her footsteps and my plants are doing well. Ferns and other acid-loving plants do love their teatime.

Green tea is a particularly good fertilizer, because it is high in nitrogen; as a bonus, the tea leaves help to ward off pests.

When potting plants, place a few used tea bags between the drainage layer at the bottom of the planter and the soil. The tea bags will help retain water, and nutrients will be leeched into the potting medium.

Banana peels contain nutrients that are particularly beneficial to roses and ferns. Cut up some peels and use them as plant food. Dry the peels before adding them to the soil so that your plants will not end up smelling like bananas.

The minerals in soda water help green leafy plants to grow. Pour about a pint into the soil once a week.

❧

A tablespoon of Epsom salts (depending on the houseplant's size) is also a good fertilizer for houseplants, as well as for roses, rhododendrons, and miniature evergreen trees.

A raw potato will give a fledgling geranium all the nutrients it needs. Carve a small hole in the potato, slip a geranium stem into it, and then plant the potato and geranium in the soil together.

❧

Be Your Own Plant Doctor

Plants are prone to insect attacks, diseases, and other physiological issues. Armed with green-thumb know-how, you can track down the cause of most ailments and correct them. For example, if your plants fail to produce flower buds, the environment is most likely the cause. Look for poor light, too low or too high a temperature, or improper nutrition. A sickly, yellowed plant is often lacking nitrogen or iron. Balanced feeding will correct this condition immediately. Leaf scorch is common among ferns and begonias. It usually is a sign of too little water, too much sun, or not enough humidity. Soft growth in the winter is usually due to a combination of high heat and insufficient light. Then, of course, there are the pests.

The most common pests are aphids, which generally appear on the tips and undersides of leaves. They often secrete a sticky white honey-dew-like substance. The best way to get rid of this secretion is to clean the plant with water mixed with a few drops of liquid dishwashing soap. Rub the afflicted area with a Q-tip to remove the aphids and their sticky substance.

Another common pest is the white fly. Use the same treatment used for aphids, and then move the afflicted plant outdoors in warm weather. The white flies will be washed away by the rain—you'll be happy to know that pests, such as aphids, spider mites, and white flies can't swim. The other, simpler option is to mist them well with a spray bottle. A watering can will also do the trick.

Other ailments include leaf rust, or *Cerotelium fici*. This disease brings about premature leaf fall and reduces fruit yields. Leaf spot results from infection by *Cylindrocladium scoparium* or *Cercospora fici*. To treat these problems, clean your plant regularly and well with soapy water, using a Q-tip and paper towels to remove the blight.

My Favorite Houseplants and Trees

Following is a list of my favorite houseplants and trees, along with guidelines for proper preparation and maintenance. You should realize before purchasing a houseplant that its lifespan may be limited. Some are appropriate for certain holiday seasons and bring a festive air. For example, paper-whites and amaryllis are especially charming to have around during the winter holidays, but they will not last indefinitely.

AFRICAN VIOLET
This beautiful flowering plant needs indirect sunlight and a warm environment. Make sure the pot has good drainage. Place water in the pot's saucer.

AMARYLLIS
This plant is easy to maintain. Plant the bulb in moist potting soil. Use a support stake to keep the stalk upright. Water regularly and place in indirect sunlight. The large buds will open four to six weeks after planting.

AZALEA
Azaleas grow outside during the summer. Transplant them into a pot filled with acidic soil in September, and enjoy them indoors for the rest of the year (they may not continue to bloom indoors).

BEGONIA
One of the most versatile houseplants, begonias like warm, indirect sunlight. Some varieties are grown for their flowers

and others for their striking foliage. Growing begonias as houseplants requires a little bit of knowledge in order to keep them looking their very best. Care of begonias indoors starts with proper location. They do best in bright, indirect light and require plenty of humidity. Experts suggest that you wait until the plant shows signs of being dry, such as drooping leaves, before you water it. This will help to prevent accidental overwatering, the main reason begonias die when grown indoors. When watering, make sure to water below the leaves in order to avoid inviting fungal disease.

CALLA LILY (both yellow and white)
These flowers need full sun and ample water.

CACTUS
This exotic plant is a type of succulent. Most cacti like bright light and a dry, sandy soil. Avoid overwatering.

CHRYSANTHEMUM
This flowering plant is easy to maintain. Just give it full sun and ample water.

CITRUS PLANTS AND TREES
Part of a large family that includes lemon, orange, lime, and kumquat, citrus plants and trees are handsome and they smell divine when in bloom. They need lots of indirect sunlight. If placed in a room that is too hot and dry, their blooming habits may be erratic. During the summer, you can take these plants and trees outside.

CYCLAMEN
Easy to grow, cyclamens need to be potted in moist soil. They also prefer full sunlight. If their leaves start to yellow, it is because of lack of light or the temperature is too hot.

EASTER LILY
I love the fragrant smell of Easter lilies. Make sure the plant receives plenty of direct sunlight. Lack of bright light can cause the leaves to yellow or root rot to develop. Although this plant should be watered regularly, about twice a week, make sure you don't overwater it.

FERNS
All ferns like a peaty and moist soil, a cool windowsill, and indirect sunlight. They thrive in humidity. In living and family rooms, stand their pots on trays filled with layers of damp pebbles or clay granules. Mist the plants regularly with tepid water unless the humidity of the whole room is kept high with a humidifier.

❧

Keep ferns in dim light so long as you give them regular breaks in bright light. Artificial light is fine provided you use a special gardening bulb. Ordinary light bulbs generate too much heat.

❧

FIG TREE

I have several fig trees in my home. Their leaves and fruit are appealing. They like ample light, a warm temperature, and not too much water.

FLOWERING MAPLE

This flowering plant, with maple-like leaves and orange-colored flowers, requires a cool environment with no direct sunlight. Too much sun can hurt its flowers.

GARDENIA

I love the luxurious scent of the gardenia, and its romantic overtones. However, this plant has its challenges. It requires full sun, a night temperature of 60°F, and a daytime temperature of 70°F to 80°F. Move your gardenia outdoors during the summer months.

GERANIUM

Geraniums like a cool temperature of around 60°F, full sunlight, and plenty of water. Water them about twice a week. Too much shade and a high temperature will result in a spindly plant. Pinch off the growing tips to make the plant bushy. Dormant geraniums can be kept during the winter months by hanging them upside down in the cellar.

HYACINTH

I like to force hyacinth bulbs in glass containers for indoor display during the winter. Set a bulb in the container so its base almost touches the water. Or, plant the bulb when its leaf tips are just showing in a soil-based potting mixture in an attractive container with drainage holes. Keep the hyacinth in a dark place at temperatures above freezing (but no higher than 45°F) for at least ten weeks to allow the roots to develop. When shoots are about 1 inch long, gradually move the plant to an area with more light and a higher temperature. Forced hyacinths do well in a room with direct sunlight at a temperature of 65°F and will flourish for several weeks. Enjoy their fragrant smell. After flowering, hyacinths may be planted in the garden; they will flower again in subsequent years.

IVY

There are many kinds of ivy—from traditional English ivy and wandering Jew to grape ivy. Most like bright windows but indirect sun. Ivies can grow in soil or in just plain water, and require a temperature of around 70°F. There's a timeless elegance to this plant. The way it trails across surfaces creates a charming effect. Plus, it's super easy to start a new plant—an instant hostess gift—with a cutting from a section of the stem. Ivy also makes a great topiary (see Topiaries on page 182).

NORFOLK ISLAND PINE

This charming indoor evergreen needs to be set in a cool spot, such as a windowsill. Moist soil is essential.

ORCHID

These exotic plants are easy to care for and their flowers last a long time. They like bright light—without sunlight, they will seldom bloom. They prefer lukewarm water once a week. Overwatering leads to the demise of many orchids. Constant wetness causes the roots to rot, which leaves the plant without a means for drawing nourishment. The leaves will subsequently droop, signaling the death of the plant. The classic advice is to water an orchid the day before it dries out, and to let the plant go dry if you are not sure whether it is time to water. Lack of water will not kill the plant. Another way to determine if water is

needed is to stick your finger in the soil. If it feels wet, no water is needed.

South- and east-facing windows work best for orchids. West windows can be too hot in the afternoon and north-facing ones are usually too dark. Too much direct light causes leaves to burn—and so it may be necessary to reposition plants as the seasons change. Move plants either away from the window or toward it to control the amount of light. Make sure the leaves are not touching the glass. In winter in a cold climate, leaves touching the windowpane may freeze. Leaf color indicates if the amount of light is adequate. The lush, rich, dark green of most houseplants is not desirable in orchid leaves. A grassy green color (light or medium green with yellowish tones) means the orchid plant is receiving sufficient light to bloom.

One of the best orchids for the home is the *Phalaenopsis* (or moth orchid). It will grow easily under the same conditions enjoyed by African violets. Another good choice is the *Paphiopedilum* (or the slipper orchid), which has attractive foliage and will reflower in ideal conditions, giving weeks of floral display. To make orchid leaves shiny, clean them with a solution of two-thirds water and one-third milk. I learned this trick at an orchid farm in the Bahamas.

PALM TREE
There are many varieties. Soak these trees well when watering, and be sure to give them filtered light. Do not overwater.

PAPER-WHITE
Belonging to the narcissus family, paper-whites are easily grown indoors in a pot or a vase. Their large clusters of pure white flowers arch above graceful, blue-green foliage, and their perfume fills a room with fragrance.

Paper-whites require no special preparation and are foolproof. Bulbs planted in early December will flower within four to six weeks.

PASSIONFLOWER
This early winter flowering plant should be placed in a cool window. Water it about once a week. In late winter give the plant more water and move it to a warmer place, about 72°F. It requires more water during the summer.

PHILODENDRON
This trailing houseplant, which is easy to maintain, loves to wend its way down from mantels or bookshelves. Its perky, dark green leaves are heart shaped. Philodendron thrives in a range of lighting conditions, from low to sunny, but does best in indirect light. Standard room temperature is ideal. Let the surface of the soil dry between waterings; do not overwater.

RUBBER TREE
This houseplant with dark green leaves that have an attractive sheen will grow into an eight-foot-tall tree, and serves as a major statement in a room. If you prefer a more shrub-like plant, shape it by pruning any long stems. Allow the surface of the soil to dry out between waterings. The tree thrives in medium to bright light, and a range of room temperatures—from about 60°F to 80°F.

SNAKE PLANT
Nicknamed the mother-in-law's tongue, this houseplant has variegated leaves that grow upright, and occasional small white flowers. Some varieties have leaves with yellow or white edges. Snake plants grow well in a wide range of lighting conditions—from medium to bright. The air in the space should be somewhat dry. Keep the soil on the dry side.

SUCCULENTS

These plants are booming in popularity for two reasons—they are fascinating and they are nearly indestructible. Technically, a succulent is any plant with thick, fleshy water-storage organs. They hold water in their leaves, stems, or roots. These plants have adapted to survive arid conditions throughout the world—from Africa to the deserts of North America. No matter what kind of succulent you're growing, the rules are pretty similar among species. Here are the general requirements: Succulents prefer bright light, such as a south-facing window. Watch the leaves for indications that the light level is correct. Some species will scorch if suddenly exposed to direct sunlight. The leaves will turn brown or white as the plant bleaches out, and the soft tissues will be destroyed. Alternatively, an underlit succulent's stem will begin to stretch, and its leaves will become widely spaced. This condition is known as etiolation. To prevent this from happening, provide better light and prune the plant back to its original shape. Many kinds of succulents will thrive outdoors in the summer.

TOPIARIES

These lovely decorative indoor and outdoor plants can last for many years if well cared for. They are architectural wonders made of living greenery, shaped and pruned by the human hand. Like so many things fashionable today, topiaries are rooted in history. The art of the topiary originated in ancient Greece, and later the Romans explored the malleability of certain plant species such as boxwood, laurel, cypress, ivy, rosemary, and myrtle to create topiary wonders. They were initially grown for the garden. The best indoor topiaries are made of ivy, rosemary, honeysuckle, laurel, and thyme.

In general, topiaries like sun and regular watering. For store-bought topiaries, examine the first inch of soil to see if it is wet or dry. Or, pop the plant out of its pot and give the roots a close look. If they appear parched, water the plant thoroughly, and then check daily to see if the surface of the soil is dry.

Most of these ornamentals need a drink at least every 3 days. Spray or mist them weekly to spritz away dust, deter pests, and add extra humidity to a dry, indoor environment. Or, give them a quick bath in the sink or tub. Topiaries growing on metal frames should be misted every day.

It is important that you provide topiaries with the proper amount of light, cool conditions, and good air circulation. East-, west-, and south-facing windows are all fine unless the sun is so strong it singes tender leaf tips.

❧

To keep topiaries fresh looking, use sharp pruning tools to trim them regularly, making sure not to cut any of the interior branches.

Add a touch of diluted fertilizer to provide the nutrients that a base filler, such as moss, lacks.

Topiaries in simple terra-cotta pots make charming displays.

You can make topiaries yourself from most herbs and evergreens. For complicated forms, a wire armature is usually needed.

❧

OPPOSITE: A traditional French way to enhance a house's entrance is with a topiary set in a French planter. Small topiaries make lovely indoor plants.

POTPOURRI

DURING THE FIRST half of the seventeenth century the French became Europe's greatest consumers of aromatics. At this time it was common practice for the French to use fragrant mixtures to scent themselves and their homes. Under the direction of the French East India Company, the planting of aromatics was begun on the French islands Île-de-France and Île Bourbon (now Mauritius and Réunion) in the Indian Ocean. The quality and variety of their produce became legendary. In France, flowers such as jasmine, violets, orange blossoms, and highly fragrant tuberoses were grown in Grasse. Along with perfumes, herbalists concocted mixtures of herbs known to repel insects and moths. They discovered that long-lasting fragrances could be produced from herbs, flowers, and spices that were mixed together and aged with fragrant oils. These herbal mixtures were placed in small bags and hung in wardrobes. They later became known as potpourri and sachets. They also helped eliminate the musty odor of drawers and closets, encouraged sleep, absorbed cooking odors, flavored culinary delights such as crème caramel with vanilla, and even soothed infants.

Making potpourri is a wonderful way to capture the bounty of your herb and flower gardens for enjoyment throughout the year. Potpourri is a colorful, dried mixture of scented flowers and aromatic leaves. Roses and lavender are ideal choices because they keep their scent for a long time. In general potpourri consists of four basic elements: dried flowers and leaves, herbs and spices, a fixative, and an essential oil. Dried flowers and leaves are the bulk of potpourri. They give the mixture color, texture, and an interesting look. If you would like a particular flower to be the focus of the potpourri, make sure it is the main component. More than one type of fragrant flower can be blended to create a mixture of color and shapes, but one fragrance will be dominant.

I love to place potpourri in open bowls around the house. Be creative and make the colors of your potpourri complement or match those in your room. You can change the atmosphere by adding a particular scent but beware that some are stronger than others. Celebrate the seasons by using different shades and scents.

Place potpourri in fabric bags (sachets) and put them in drawers and closets to scent clothing. Also, put them in storage boxes, chests, and musty cupboards to create pleasant aromas. And, tie them to doorknobs. Don't overdue it. Squeeze the sachet occasionally to release the scent. However you choose to use a potpourri, you will find it uplifts your spirit.

Drying Flowers for Potpourri

Rose and other petals and flowers for potpourri should be dried in a dust-free environment with good ventilation and away from direct sunlight. Lay the petals and whole small flowers on gauze stretched over a frame so that the air can circulate around them. In a pinch, they can be laid on newspaper, but they need to be turned occasionally. Make sure that the petals do not overlap.

Allow 4 to 7 days for small flowers to dry and up to 3 weeks for thick petals. The ideal temperature for the first day is 90°F and then 75°F after that. Small rosebuds and thick petals will need to be turned once or twice. Some flowers, such as lavender, chamomile, delphinium, and larkspur, can be dried on the stem. I like to hang them upside down in small bunches of no more than ten stems.

Cleanliness is a priority during drying and storage. Store the dried petals and flowers in glass jars, labeled with the name and date. Keep the jars in a dark spot in order to make sure that their contents do not fade.

POTPOURRI TIPS

❧ Gather suitable plants for making potpourri throughout the year.

❧ Store dried potpourri materials in a dry place in containers with lids.

❧ Never use metal bowls to hold or mix the potpourri as the metal could destroy the pleasant fragrance. Wooden, glass, ceramic, or odor-free plastic bowls are the best for stirring the mixture. Baskets and either enamel or ceramic bowls are ideal to hold it.

❧ Combine crushed or powdered spices in one bowl and oils in another. Then add them to the mixture.

❧ Citrus pips (seeds) and blossoms can be crushed and dried to serve as a fixative.

❧ Take appropriate care when handling essential oils. Some oils can increase sensitivity to light if spilled on your skin, and others can cause allergic reactions. Know the qualities of the oils you are using.

❧ For a decorative touch, pick out some of the dried flower buds and place them on top.

❧ Keep leftover potpourri in a dark container for future use.

❧ Keep potpourri away from children and pets. It can be toxic if ingested. If you are concerned, place potpourri in a container with a strong snap-on lid that lets out the scent but is impossible for small fingers or paws to pry open.

❧ To prevent potpourri from fading, don't expose it to bright sunlight.

There are many potpourri recipes. I've provided five easy-to-make seasonal potpourris that I adore, along with suggestions about making your own potpourri (see pages 187–88). Follow the directions for Old-Fashioned Rose Potpourri for all of them unless otherwise specified.

Making Your Own
POTPOURRI

Be creative and come up with your own scents. Choose a dominant smell.

1. Select from different types of flowers, leaves, herbs, roots, and spices, and even citrus peels, such as orange, lemon, lime, or tangerine. Spices, roots, and peels will give your potpourri extra depth. Crush or grind fresh spices with a mortar and pestle, or grate nutmeg to release its aroma (leave a few whole for textural interest).

2. Dry peels add zest to potpourri. To dry peels, remove a thin layer of fruit peel with a zester, grater, or potato peeler, avoiding any white skin. Dry the peel outside in the sun or in an oven set at a very low temperature. Crush or mince it if you desire.

3. An essential ingredient is the fixative. The one I prefer is orris root. You can find it in most health food stores. Use about 1 tablespoon per cup of flowers and leaves.

4. Essential oil gives potpourri a little more fragrance.

5. Pour the potpourri mixture in a sealed container in a warm, dry area for 6 weeks to cure. When ready, place the potpourri in a bowl and finger it to release the fragrance.

OLD-FASHIONED ROSE POTPOURRI

Old-fashioned French recipes for rose potpourri (referred to as "rose bowls") always call for rose petals. This concoction is based on my grandmother's heavenly potpourri. Place the potpourri in a lovely display bowl or cup.

8 cups fragrant rose petals, dried (if possible, use the 'Geranium Red' rose as it mimics the scent of the rose geranium)
3 cups rose geranium leaves, dried
½ cup orris root powder (as a fixative)
3 drops rose essential oil
2 drops rose geranium essential oil

1. Combine all the ingredients, except for the essential oils, in a large mixing bowl.

2. Add the fixative and stir thoroughly. Discard any moist pieces.

3. Add the oils, drop by drop, stirring constantly so as to distribute them evenly.

4. Place the potpourri mixture in an airtight container, and cure in a dark and dry place for 6 weeks or more. Shake the container from time to time to help redistribute the ingredients evenly.

5. When ready, put the potpourri in a small bowl.

6. When the scent begins to fade, top with a few drops of essential oils and shake the potpourri up. Add additional potpourri as needed.

SUMMER GARDEN POTPOURRI

Capture the essence of summer with this fragrant potpourri. Following are suggested combinations and quantities of flowers, dried leaves, and spices.

8 cups of any of the following (or a combination of): rose petals and buds, lavender, deep blue delphinium petals, whole lilies (or separated into petals)

½ cup of either dried rosemary leaves or small bay leaves

1 whole pink clove

1 tablespoon nutmeg

1 tablespoon ginger

5 tablespoons orris root powder (as a fixative)

NOTE: Skip Step 3.

CITRUS POTPOURRI

This potpourri has an uplifting scent that helps to alleviate stale and unpleasant smells. Citrus is ideal because it isn't too sweet or heady. This potpourri can last a long time if you refresh it with essential oil.

8 cups of any of the following (or a combination): lemon leaves, lemon verbena, lemon-scented tea tree, lemon thyme, lemon-scented geranium (*pelargonium*), and/or lemon grass

1 cup calendula petals (available at health food stores)

½ cup each orange and lemon peel

1 cup allspice, crushed lightly

1 cup orris root powder (as a fixative)

3 to 4 drops mint essential oil

6 to 8 drops lemon verbena essential oil

3 to 4 drops bergamot essential oil

FALL ROSE POTPOURRI

Here's a perfect way to extend the life of your roses. Dry out rose petals and add them to this potpourri. Kick the fragrance up a notch by adding a few drops of essential oil.

Dry rose petals from a dozen roses

¼ cup whole cloves

1 cup whole allspice

Ten 3-inch cinnamon sticks, broken into pieces

8 small bay leaves

4 whole nutmeg

3 tablespoons star anise

2 tablespoons whole cardamom pods

2 tablespoons orris root powder (as a fixative)

2 to 3 drops rose essential oil

NOTE: Skip Step 3 unless you are using essential oil.

CHRISTMAS POTPOURRI

Bring the spirit of Christmas into your home with this aromatic potpourri. Place this potpourri in a festive holiday bowl.

2 cups cedar tips, fresh or dried

1 cup bay leaves, fresh or dried

3 small pomegranates, dried

1 to 2 dried orange slices

¾ cup orange peel, dried

¼ to ½ cup cinnamon pieces, crushed

2 dozen assorted pinecones, various sizes

¼ cup rosehips, dried

2 tablespoons orris root powder (as a fixative)

4 drops cinnamon essential oil

2 drops bergamot essential oil

1 drop rosemary essential oil

Chapter Five

ENTERTAINING
AT HOME WITH
FLAIR

Home entertaining with flair requires establishing an inviting atmosphere for your guests. For me, setting up for a traditional dinner party can be as much fun as the event itself. I always start with a cocktail hour so that by the time guests sit down for the meal they are relaxed. Now, let the party begin.

If you want your event to be stress free, plan ahead and take care of the following essentials well in advance. First, make a guest list that brings together a dynamic group of people. A little controversy is good to shake up things. Do not invite too many lawyers—remember, this is not a legal conference. And, do not invite too many doctors—this is not a medical convention. Second, create a party menu to fit the occasion. Never choose a recipe that you have not mastered.

Make sure your place is tidied up a few days before. It should be sparkling. Most importantly, straighten up all the public rooms. Fluff up the pillows on the sofa, and check for any debris behind them. Thoroughly vacuum the carpet. Clean the powder room—add fresh hand towels and make sure there is extra toilet paper on hand. You do not want your guests to have to hunt for it. Make the beds the morning of the event.

❧

Hire help if it's within your budget. A bartender and a server/dishwasher are recommended.

Be dressed and ready before guests arrive. No one wants to be waiting for the host or hostess; this does not set the right tone.

When guests arrive, take their coats and bags and place them in a coat closet or a spare room in an organized fashion.

❧

An elegant dining room tablesetting *à la française.*

THE COCKTAIL HOUR

MAKE YOUR GUESTS feel welcome. Introduce everyone, and be sure when you do to include a complimentary comment about who they are and/or what they do. If there is an awkward silence after you have made an introduction, help your friends along by letting them know, in a flattering way, what they have in common. Don't be bossy. Try to avoid making statements like "You must meet" or "Please shake hands." No one likes to be told what to do, especially in a party context. After making introductions, offer each of your guests the drink of his or her choice. During the cocktail hour, play background music. I suggest compiling a playlist of French standards by Edith Piaf or hits by Carla Bruni. Drinking while talking (or even dancing) is enjoyable.

Setting Up the Bar

Setting up the bar is key to successful entertaining. Do not serve too much alcohol or food to your guests before dinner as you want to make sure that they have an appetite. I set out bowls full of nuts (I prefer hazelnuts), edamame, and radishes with sea salt, which are always appreciated.

EQUIPMENT
A tray for serving drinks should be readily available. A polished silver tray is best as it is impervious to rings from cold bottles or glasses. A range of glassware is essential—from crystal tumblers (heavy in your hand is perfect for whiskey) to stem glasses in different sizes. Cocktails are best served in small 2-to-3-ounce glasses, not in giant fishbowls. You want your guests to be happy, not sloppy. Other necessary pieces of equipment include a medium-size ice bucket (one made of crystal or silver is elegant), a few stirrers, a silver shaker, and a small plate for sliced and quartered lemon and limes. Select brightly colored cocktail napkins in fun patterns, and make them readily available.

How to Mix the Perfect French Cocktail

To concoct a great cocktail, make sure to match the glass temperature to the drink: cold drinks go in frozen glasses. Chill a few glasses ahead of time by filling them with ice, or put them headfirst into an ice bucket until you are ready to pour. Chilled cocktail glasses will keep mixed drinks cooler longer.

If you don't have a designated bartender, invite your guests to make their own drinks. Just be sure that you have laid out all the necessary supplies ahead of time.

KIR

Kir (originally called *vin blanc cassis*) became the cocktail of choice in French cafes in the mid-nineteenth century. Félix Kir, the mayor of Dijon in Burgundy, further popularized the drink after World War II. He served it so often to promote his region's wine and crème de cassis (black currant liqueur), the name "Kir" has been associated with it ever since. There are many variations of this cocktail. The crème de cassis or *liqueur de framboise* acts as as a sweetener for your favorite wine or champagne.

LIQUOR, WINE, AND SOFT DRINKS

Always have the following beverages available:

- An array of whiskey (Irish, bourbon, and Scotch), gin, vodka, rum, and dry vermouth, along with any special type of liquor that your friends enjoy, along with mixers, such as tonic, ginger ale, and bitters.

- A bottle of chilled white wine (opened or ready to be) and a bottle of red wine. I usually serve red wine with dinner. Chilled champagne is a chic addition.

- Bottles of Perrier or San Pellegrino for nondrinkers.

FLORAL ICE CUBES
for Warm-Weather Entertaining

Sweet violets and nasturtium can be captured in ice cubes and used as a garnish for cool drinks. Place the flowers face down in the base of the individual cubes of an ice-cube tray. Add water, and then freeze. If you have difficulty keeping the flowers in position, put a little water on the top and freeze. Then fill the ice-cube tray completely and freeze again.

KIR COCKTAILS

KIR

¼ ounce crème de cassis
2¼ ounces dry white wine

Pour the crème de cassis into a wine glass, and then slowly add the dry white wine.

KIR ROYALE

¼ ounce crème de cassis
2¼ ounces of champagne

Pour the crème de cassis into a champagne glass, and then slowly add the champagne.

KIR BRETON

¼ ounce crème de cassis
2¼ ounces Breton cider

Pour the crème de cassis into a wine glass, and then slowly add the cider.

KIR IMPÉRIAL

¼ ounce crème de framboise
(raspberry liqueur)
2¼ ounces champagne

Pour the raspberry liqueur in a champagne flute, and then slowly add the champagne.

THE FRENCH MARTINI

One of the most popular cocktails is the martini. The glass itself is the ultimate in sophistication. Following is a French twist on this legendary drink.

2 ounces gin
1 ounce dry vermouth
Dash of orange bitters
Lemon twists

1. Pour the gin over ice in a tall shaker.

2. Add the dry vermouth and a dash of orange bitters.

3. Stir like crazy, until your shaker is sweating.

4. Run a lemon twist around the edge of the glass, and then pour your elixir into the glass through a strainer.

5. Add a lemon twist by grasping both ends, gently turning hands in opposite directions until it spritzes into your cocktail. Then drop it in.

SETTING THE TABLE

FROM THE IMPOSING trestle table of the Middle Ages to my grandmother's holiday spread, the table setting has always been a principal part of entertaining. Styles have changed throughout the centuries. Dining tools and accessories have evolved. Tablecloths now run the gamut from pristine white to bright and colorful hues and patterns. The fashions for different styles of pottery, china, and porcelain have also changed. They now range from fine Sèvres to whimsical pottery. And, silverware has morphed into silver plate. The constant is that a beautiful table is still a treat to behold.

In my opinion, setting a beautiful table is an art form. The table setting not only conveys a mood but also frames the food being served. When you are having a great time at a dinner party, it is rarely simply because the food is tasty. Stepping into a room with a lovely table setting gives the impression of good things to come. It shows that you care and have made an effort on behalf of your guests. Often a glorious setting can bring simple fare to the next level. Gather elements to set a particular scene—from selecting the right napkins and plates to enhancing them with the sparkle of glasses and the shine of the silverware. Do not save your good china, glasses, and silver for special occasions. Make anytime special and use what you have. Even better—mix styles to create a more personal tablescape.

ABOVE: Artichokes served on chic contrasting plates make a lovely appetizer. The silverware is set *à l'anglaise.*

Set an attractive table ahead of time. You do not want to be finishing up as your guests arrive. But first, make sure that your dining area is warm (not too hot) and has flattering light (see Candlesticks and Candelabras on page 217). No one will enjoy their food and the company if there is a draft. Lower the temperature a bit to take into consideration the body heat generated by several people. It is also important to assign seats to your guests. I try to seat boy/girl and I always separate a husband and wife. You want your guests to meet new people and to have lively conversations.

When it comes to forks, spoons, and knives, there is a "right" way to lay them on the table. The concentration of cutlery and glassware on the right-hand side of the plate is thought to have originated in France, with the idea that you should hold your napkin with your left hand and eat with your right. The conventional rule is that the fork should be on the left, and the knife and soup spoon on the right.

All utensils and glasses are organized in order of use—from the outside in. If soup is the first course, the soup spoons are placed to the far right of the knives, unless a small shellfish fork is needed for the first course. A dessert fork and spoon may be placed horizontally above the dinner plate.

There are a few variations when it comes to glassware, but generally the water goblet is placed directly above the knife, a champagne flute just to the left, and the red and/or white wine glass to the right. Some people prefer to arrange their glasses by height. Just be sure they're lined up, and slightly curved toward the guest, not creeping toward the adjacent diner.

The bread plate (optional) is placed directly across from the glasses, aligned over the forks.

To ensure guests have adequate elbow room, established rules of etiquette dictate that there should be a minimum of 15 inches between place settings, or approximately 24 inches from the center of one place setting to the middle of the next.

Make sure that your guests will never be without a plate in front of them. Two plates on top of one another will make the service easier. Besides, stacked plates of varying sizes also look good on the table. Or, you can put the soup bowl on top of the plate that will be used for the next course. The same goes for the salad plate if you start with a salad.

To make serving easier, have a pitcher filled with cold water on the table before everyone is seated. Or, even better, fill everyone's water glasses before you sit down. Place salt and pepper on the table ahead of time, too, along with wine, bread, butter, or olive oil. This will save you unnecessary trips to the kitchen during dinner.

Tableware

POTTERY: PORCELAIN, FAIENCE, AND EARTHENWARE

For me, a refined table exhibits a mixture of styles and designs, often from different periods. The tableau should be playful and very personal. Besides, a mixture is more affordable than a matched set. The effect will look wonderful, especially if you stick to a theme or a color. A wide variety of plates and serving pieces can be found at flea markets, auctions, and antiques shops. Educate yourself about the differences and kinds of pottery, such as porcelain, faience, and earthenware (see below).

In French homes of the past, it was typical to have several complete sets of porcelain (consisting of dozens of pieces or more), received as a wedding present, inherited, or bought throughout the years. Young brides had their trousseaus, and bridegrooms had their porcelain and faience. Sets of dinnerware consisted of dinner plates, soup plates, and dessert plates, along with assorted vegetable dishes, meat and fish serving plates, tureens, and bowls. Today, it is more fun and economical to buy porcelain in small batches and to create an interesting mix and match of patterns. However, most people seem to prefer faience and earthenware to porcelain as they are more casual and whimsical and often more suited to today's lifestyle.

Porcelain and earthenware plates are available in many shapes, colors, and designs. I love them not only for their beauty but also for the memories they evoke: Sunday lunches at my parents' or my grandmother's homes, holidays in Brittany or Normandy, picnics on the lawn or at the beach, and lunches at my cousins'.

Porcelain

This dishware is fine and fragile, made from a combination of clays—kaolin, quartz, and feldspar—fired at a very high temperature to harden it. There are two main types:

HARD-PASTE (*pâte dure*) porcelain is made from white china clay and a rock called china stone. It was first made in China in 8 CE and later in Europe at the beginning of the eighteenth century. Meissen and other factories in Germany created some beautiful and colorful examples starting around 1709. The French Sèvres factory started to produce it on a grand scale around 1758, and continues to do so today.

SOFT-PASTE (*pâte tendre*) porcelain, which is an imitation of true porcelain, was invented in Europe as a substitute before the secret of "real" porcelain was discovered in Europe. Saint-Cloud, Chantilly, and then Vincennes factories produced exquisite examples as early as 1673. Factories opened up in English locations such as Chelsea and Derby but production stopped at the end of the eighteenth century. Therefore, soft-paste porcelain is much rarer than hard-paste and so is a favorite among collectors.

When porcelain is perfect, its ringing sound is clear. When broken and restored, it sounds dull.

Faience

Faience is the French name for lead-glazed or tin-glazed earthenware that is richly decorated and colored. It also refers to German, Scandinavian, Spanish, and Italian wares. Some of my favorites are asparagus or oyster plates from the French Sarreguemines factory, but plates from Gien are also beautiful. Recently there has been a revival of interest in barbotine ware, an early European ware decorated with raised slip designs. Luneville and Saint-Clement faience are still affordable, while prices for Choisy are on the rise and Vallauris is deservedly sought after due to its fine quality. When you buy barbotine ware, select pieces that are in mint condition. As a general rule, the heavier the relief, the older the piece.

Faience can be distinguished from porcelain in several ways. In terms of appearance, porcelain is thin and translucent, while faience is matte and opaque. In terms of feel, porcelain is regular and the enameling is uniform, while faience is irregular to the touch. And in terms of sound, porcelain sounds crystalline when tapped, while faience emits a muted sound.

Earthenware

Earthenware is clay fired at a low temperature, making it quite porous. Often artisanal, it is thick, heavy, and easily chipped.

STORAGE AND CARE OF POTTERY

Storage

By storing pottery in an accessible cupboard in the kitchen or in the dining room, you will use it often. I cannot think of anything prettier than a sideboard or shelves full of mismatched vintage china. It is far more interesting to collect individual pieces than to buy a complete, brand-new set.

To store your fine porcelain plates or faience, put a piece of paper in between each plate and dish. The paper will protect them from damaging each other.

Cleaning and Repairing

Here are ways to clean off stains and grease marks from a beloved piece of pottery.

To repair a crack in a porcelain or faience piece, turn to a professional. However, with some skill, you can master the art of pottery repair.

My Method for
STAIN REMOVAL

1. Rinse the piece of pottery under running warm water.

2. Apply a mixture of one part water and one part white vinegar to the stain. Add some baking soda for difficult stains.

3. Then place the pottery in a plastic bag for 30 minutes before rinsing it in water.

4. Dry the piece carefully with a soft cloth.

My Method for
GREASE REMOVAL

1. Soak the piece of pottery in hot water with organic soap for 20 minutes.

2. Carefully remove the grease marks with a hard bristle brush or scrubby.

3. Rinse the pottery in cold water, and dry it with a soft cloth.

4. Place the pottery in an oven at 200°F for ½ hour. For persistent marks, repeat this process.

My Method for
REPAIRING A CRACK

1. Clean the crack with a Q-tip and soapy water without submerging the piece. If this is not sufficient to clean the crack, rub it with a Q-tip dipped in a solution of one part acetone and two parts water.

2. Carefully rinse the piece, and gently dry with a soft cloth.

3. Using a toothpick, apply epoxy glue along the crack.

4. Place the piece in the oven at 200°F for 5 minutes. This will make the crack open wide enough to draw in the glue.

5. Remove the piece from the oven, and clean off the excess glue with a rag dipped in rubbing alcohol.

6. Apply tape around the piece to set it in place.

7. Put the piece back in the oven for 10 more minutes.

8. Take the piece out of the oven and set it aside in a safe place to cool.

Always dry items by laying them carefully on a folded towel near the sink.

Never submerge mended pieces of china in water because doing so will weaken the adhesive. Instead, rinse them and let them air-dry.

Silverware

....

The distinctive quality of silver has been recognized throughout the ages. Silver is a symbol of wealth and status. In medieval times people served themselves from a common plate using their hands. Two or three people sipped soup from the same bowl. Bread and meat were dipped in a single salt cellar. In the late eleventh century when a certain Byzantine princess arrived in Venice to marry the doge, she ate her food with a golden fork, and the bishop reprimanded her for not eating with her hands. It was not until the Renaissance that the fork came into use—but then, it was only for lifting morsels from one's plate.

The first forks appeared mainly in southern Europe during the thirteenth and fourteenth centuries and were used primarily for sweet foods (fruits in syrup). This type of fork, often carried together with a spoon and toothpick, was a personal object rather than one provided by a host for his guest. A revolution in table manners came in the fifteenth century in Italy, when the fork replaced fingers as the main tool for eating. Interestingly, at the time, knives, forks, and spoons were made of brass, rarely of silver. From the sixteenth century on, the

A collection of antique dessert spoons, forks, and fruit knives with their storage box.

use of one's fingers for eating was increasingly discouraged in most European countries. By the seventeenth century (and a bit later in England), each aristocratic or wealthy person had his own plate, glass, knife, spoon, and fork, which they brought with them when they went to someone else's house. Silver or silver gilt were the materials of choice. In order to prevent servants and untrustworthy guests from stealing them, silver forks, spoons, and other utensils were marked with the owner's initials or crest.

By the eighteenth century dining had become a pretext for a complex social ritual, with certain formal steps, much like ballet. Eating with others was a highly developed social skill. The use of diverse utensils required specific training. For example, food was not to be placed in the mouth with the tip of the knife. Spoons came in a variety of shapes—there were stew spoons, coffee spoons, spoons for entremets, and so on. One had to learn which utensil was proper to use —and how to use it—to be accepted in society. To this day, the absence of good table manners is the kiss of death in most social circles. And, children are often scolded by their parents for eating with their fingers, which is deemed unsanitary.

In the late seventeenth century forks took on the shape that we know today. However, there is a long and interesting history—from the primitive pick to the contemporary three- or four-pronged utensil. In France the fork was held in the right hand (provided that one was right-handed) and used as a pick. Americans also used the fork with the right hand, but they often spooned their food up with it. Then there is the complicated matter of different kinds of forks for fish, meat, salad, and dessert. Which fork is to be used for what kind of food? Meat

Silverware comes in many forms. Saltcellars bring a touch of old world elegance to the table.

necessitated forks that were simpler, stronger, and larger than forks (or "suckets") designed for sweet morsels. The first meat fork had two or three prongs, but before the end of the seventeenth century, the four-pronged type was common.

A relatively small number of antique silverware and other pieces has survived in part due to the relatively soft nature of the metal (and its intrinsic value). Despite its worth, a shaky hinge or a dent makes a piece of antique silver less valuable. That combined with individuals' urgent need for cash throughout history has made these pieces candidates for the melting pot. Even monarchs resorted to melting down their silver pieces. The French King Louis XIV, for example, had valuable silver items in Versailles's Galerie des Glaces that he had to have melted down around 1685 in order to raise much-needed cash.

It is interesting to note that even today the finest silver is still chiefly handmade.

Silver accessories—from sugar and cheese spoon, and grape scissors to a teapot and salad servers with ivory prongs—are wonderful collectibles that can be used to create a sophisticated table.

However, many variations in quality exist, allowing silver to be more affordable. Even machine-made pieces have become fashionable. This occurrence was the result of several factors: the discovery of Nevada's Comstock Lode, which lowered the cost of silver ore; the invention of electroplating; and mass production. Because of the rising middle class there was a market for these newly available wares. The middle class strove to emulate the extravagant lifestyle of the upper class. In fact, endless etiquette books provided the upwardly mobile hostess with precise information on how to give a proper dinner party using all sorts of silverware.

Engraved silverware handed down through the generations, or bought at auction (see Collecting Silverware on page 209), gives immediate elegance to a dinner table. I have inherited lovely sets from my grandmother, along with tea and coffee services, which I cherish and use all the time. However, for everyday use, most people prefer flatware that is not made of a precious metal. This more casual alternative is often crafted out of cast aluminum, and does not require monogramming to keep thieves at bay. Alternatively, silver-plated eating utensils are ideal for everyday use, and over time, they acquire the rich warm patina of prized heirlooms.

SERVING UTENSILS

Silver serving utensils are not only useful but also truly wonderful. They come in a broad range of sizes and shapes and add an elegant touch to the table. In the nineteenth century there were no dishes or desserts that didn't have their own special serving tools. You can still find "hors d'oeuvre sets," meat-carving utensils, fish servers, asparagus tongs, sugar spoons, strawberries spoons, cheese and dessert servers, and much more.

❧

A big silver ladle is the most useful spoon for a steaming stew or a tureen of soup.

A salad is much easier to serve with a pair of salad servers.

❧

COLLECTING SILVERWARE

Part of the charm of old things is that they are not perfect. You will appreciate the beauty of silverware even more if each piece is slightly different. Enjoy the hunt—during the warm weather, visit country fairs, shop at antiques stores and flea markets, and attend auctions. Invest in your very own heirloom collection, and in turn embellish your dinner table with style.

As a rule, complete sets of knives, forks, and spoons are expensive. My advice is to select a model and then assemble a set piece by piece. Or, collect different pieces and create your own unique antique set. Look for charming oddities, such as berry spoons, grape shears, bonbon scoops, or olive spears. Small sets of unusual silver hors d'oeuvre or dessert services with wood or mother-of-pearl handles can be a bargain. Carving knives and salad forks and spoons with ebony or horn handles are also affordable. Another option is

to assemble a vintage set from a grand hotel, an ocean liner, or a railway company. Hotel flatware of the past was designed to withstand constant use, and for this reason, the layer of silver with which it was plated is often thicker than what is usual. The downside is that these pieces are often worn or dented.

Invest in a book that explains silver hallmarks. This important reference will help you determine the value of silver pieces. Check the condition of each piece carefully. Keep in mind that good-quality flatware is desirable. Here are a few guidelines.

❧

When cutlery was first monogrammed in France during the late seventeenth century, the crest or the initials were always placed on the reverse side. In England and in America it is just the opposite. This explains why the French always lay their forks with the prongs facedown on the tablecloth (this is much safer as you will not hurt yourself); the Anglo-Saxons do just the opposite.

Forks should have straight prongs, with no ends missing. They should not be too heavy, too big, or too sharp.

Look for knives with interesting handles. Search for one-off pieces in amber, horn, porcelain, mother-of-pearl, or wood. Check each knife for sharpness and ensure that it is properly weighted. Heavier handles are best. The handles of knives should be joined. Sometimes it is an easy repair to reglue the handles.

Large spoons are often more available than large forks.

❧

STORAGE AND CARE OF SILVERWARE

Storage

Silverware should be stored in the dark in pouches. Chamois is ideal, or tissue paper will do. Another option is in an empty silver chest or a special drawer for silverware. My grandmother always placed a piece of chalk in the drawer to prevent her silverware from tarnishing. Make sure not to use rubber bands to hold silverware or small pieces with several parts together (such as a sugar bowl with its lid and spoon) as the rubber will stain the surface.

Cleaning

Silver and silver plate can be put in the dishwasher if the pieces are not mixed with items made of steel or aluminum, which will tarnish it. Carefully dry after washing to remove lingering stains (see how to polish silver pieces on page 112).

Knives with horn, ivory, tortoiseshell, or any kind of glued-on handle must be washed by hand. They should not be soaked.

Acidic substances, including lemon or vinegar, will tarnish silver.

Crystal and Everyday Glassware

The finest of all glassware is lead crystal. It is made with lead, or a similar chemical element, that is heated at a very high temperature, and is often hand blown, etched, or engraved. Glass has to be at least 24 percent lead to carry the lead crystal appellation. More lead gives weight and increases the sparkle. Everyday glassware is made with soda lime—a combination of limestone and silica.

During the first century BCE, the Syrians invented the art of glassblowing, which spread quickly throughout the Roman Empire and beyond. During the seventeenth and eighteenth centuries, Italy, Bohemia, and England successively dominated the European glass trade before France finally had its turn in the nineteenth century. French craftsmen began producing beautiful crystal glasses, which came to adorn not only the aristocratic French tables but also tables of the czars, emperors, and maharajahs. My grandmother's closet was filled with these glorious glasses, which were only brought out for holidays or special occasions. She had complete sets of water tumblers, glasses for red and white wine, flutes and coupes for champagne, and all sorts of liquor glasses, made by either Baccarat or Saint-Louis (considered by many to be the best crystal suppliers).

Until the eighteenth century glasses were not set on the dining table but instead on a side table, where they were kept in glass holders or coolers. Diners asked servants to bring them glasses of wine (which were often diluted with water) and in turn handed back their empty glasses. A special drinking cup—sometimes called an *orgue du plaisir* (organ of pleasure)—was shared by all.

From about 1880 on, diners were each provided with a set of three to six glasses of the same pattern, which were positioned in a rectangular formation above the plate and accompanied by matching carafes. Times have changed.

The art of laying an elegant table is much more relaxed than in the past. Glasses are the jewels of a table, reflecting the light and contributing to a room's ambience. A host can now mix all sorts of glasses—from crystal to pressed glass and from absinthe to beer mugs—and use them as he or she wishes. Few of us have full sets of anything, which to my mind is fine. It is so much more elegant to mix shapes and styles. As far as I am concerned, small glasses are ideal. Low tumblers with stubby stems are wonderful for water as are Moroccan tea glasses. Sherry glasses are a lovely alternative for wine. One thing I detest are gigantic balloon wine glasses that seemingly hold a whole bottle's worth of wine. Stay away from them. Colored glasses add a festive touch to a table.

Never fill a glass to the brim. Fill wine and water glasses halfway or less and refill them as needed.

An attentive host is one who never lets a guest end up with an empty glass.

COLLECTING FINE CRYSTAL AND OTHER GLASSWARE
Crystal glasses manufactured today cost much more than the same design bought second-hand. You can distinguish crystal from glass by the sound. Crystal sounds "crystalline," and hence is named after a bell. It is heavier than glass and more transparent.

To determine whether or not a glass is old, pass your fingers under its foot. If it feels uneven, the glass is old. The foot is smooth on anything made from the nineteenth century on. Another telltale sign is that old glass is irregular, with bubbles and imperfections.

Red wine glasses and water glasses are much more sought after than white wine, port, or liquor glasses (which are used less often).

Pressed glass is beautiful. It always carries the vertical impression of the joints of its mold.

GLASSWARE CARE

Crystal glasses can be cleaned in the dishwasher if they are washed alone in a light cycle using a gentle detergent. Antique glassware demands special care. Wash these pieces individually by hand; never put them all together in the sink as they are fragile. Line the sink with a dishtowel for padding, and do not use hot water as it may crack the antique glass. Add a cupful of white vinegar to the rinsing water to enhance their shine.

❧

Colored glasses should not be washed in the dishwasher as the color will fade.

❧

Napkins and Tablecloths

Napkins and tablecloths are important, along with silverware, glass, and china, to create an attractive and inviting tableau. Here are my tips for proper use and care of these fine elements so that they decorate your table for many years.

NAPKINS

The ancient Greeks were the first to use napkins—if you can call them that. They wiped their hands with lumps of dough. This practice evolved during the Middle Ages, when diners used slices of bread to wipe their hands. Eventually they cleaned their hands on tablecloths as the old practices faded away and stricter rules regarding table manners took hold.

Around 1660 in France napkins came into vogue and guests were no longer expected to wipe their fingers on the tablecloth. Crisp starched linen damask or rich indiennes covered dining tables that were enhanced by assorted napkins. Manuals from this period provide many ways of folding napkins into fanciful shapes. Napkin art reached its zenith under Louis XIV at Versailles, where napkin folding was a profession. Today, napkin folding is not nearly as elaborate.

Until the nineteenth century common practice was to tuck your napkin into your collar to protect your clothing from stains. The fashion changed because of social mores and diners began to drape their napkins over their knees. It is still perfectly acceptable to use a napkin as a bib for certain foods—for example, lobster, which is particularly messy.

For me, a good napkin should be large—the bigger the better. It should cover your knees, even when folded in half. Most of my napkins are made of linen and belonged to my mother or grandmother. They come in different colors and are soft because they've been laundered many times. Mix and match napkins. Look for interesting patterns. Vintage ones (if you can get your hands them) are the Rolls-Royce of napkins, especially white linen ones with embroidered initials. Large French dishcloths also make brilliant napkins. Search auction houses and tag sales and cobble together a mismatched set. I also like brightly colored linen or cotton ones. I prefer to place the napkin to the right of the spoon. Most Europeans do it this way. In the United States the napkin is placed to the left of the place setting. For informal meals you can put the napkin wherever you choose, such as on top of the dinner plate. I often use napkin rings. For special events, I like to tie ribbons around napkins or to wrap them with foliage.

Napkin Sizes

- OLD-FASHIONED-STYLE napkins are square or rectangular.
- DINNER NAPKINS are large: 31 or 28 inches square, or often 18 inches square.
- TEA NAPKINS are small: 12 inches square.
- COCKTAIL NAPKINS are very small: 9 inches square, 4 by 6 inches, or 6 by 8 inches.

TABLECLOTHS

The tablecloth dresses up a table and makes it look festive. Besides unifying the table setting, it also insulates the table, lowering the noise level in the room.

Roman emperors are credited with introducing tablecloths. Banquet tables were draped in opulent fabrics that pooled on the floor. From antiquity on, tablecloths became synonymous with luxurious eating. They were a way to show off wealth and hospitality, and to mark a special meal. By the tenth century, the tablecloth had spread through the Byzantine Empire and feudal Western Europe, and evolved into the large table covering that we know today. In the fourteenth century it became customary to use tablecloths made of the finest white linen. The higher your station, the whiter your tablecloths were expected to be. At the time linen was valuable and expensive. It had to be harvested, handspun, bleached, and then handwoven into cloth. Furthermore, linen had to be carefully maintained—from washing it to pressing it. Considered a family heirloom, linen was often displayed either in a linen press or stacked in a place where it could be seen by visitors.

In eighteenth-century France rules for tablecloth etiquette in aristocratic circles were not only practical but involved. Tablecloths in proper households had to be layered so that the top one could be removed after the first course to reveal a pristine one for the second. The tablecloth had to be 16 inches from the floor. Today such rigid rules are no longer necessary for a good-looking table. However, a tablecloth still signifies that a meal is special and that your guests are worth making an effort for.

Tablecloth Sizes

- For a formal dinner, the tablecloth overhang should be deep, approximately 10 to 15 inches—a drop that rests in the diner's lap and is tucked under the table before the napkin is lifted.
- To calculate the yardage for a tablecloth, measure the length and width of the table, the overhang, and the hem allowance.
- For a buffet table, partly because no one sits at it, the overhang may be generous, even hanging to the floor.

NAPKIN AND TABLECLOTH ETIQUETTE

- Napkins should be used to wipe your fingers and blot your lips as needed (and always after taking a drink)—not to blow your nose.
- After sitting, unfold your napkin and place it in your lap. Do not tuck it in your collar (see page 212 for exceptions).

If leaving the table during the meal, place your napkin on your chair. When the meal is finished, fold your napkin loosely, and place it in the center of your place setting if your plate has been cleared.

Do not clean your hands, face, cutlery, or anything else on a tablecloth. This is what a napkin is for.

NAPKIN AND TABLECLOTH CARE

Soiled napkins and tablecloths need to be laundered the day after the dinner party (or if possible, immediately after the party). Otherwise the stains will set and become harder to remove. Wash them on a delicate cycle (see further washing information on page 127). Never store linens in a dry, hot attic or a damp cellar. Instead, put them in a linen closet or a chest of drawers (see page 127).

PLACE MATS

Place mats—an informal alternative to a tablecloth—are a modern invention. Designed to accommodate plates, glasses, and silverware, place mats protect a table surface from being damaged. In my opinion, they should be used for small gatherings or for casual luncheons or dinners. They look delightful on a wooden table with a lovely finish. They are equally pleasing on a marble or glass surface. Place mats come in various shapes, including rectangular, oval, and round. You can find them in paper, painted cardboard, cloth, with embroidery and beading, and much more. To avoid a messy look, carefully set place mats relative to the edge of the table (this will vary due to a table's size and shape). To provide adequate elbowroom, allow a minimum of 4 inches between place mats.

Candlesticks and Candelabras

Dinner by candlelight adds allure to a party. I use candles when throwing a dinner party because the table and guests look glorious in candlelight. Its flickering light helps to create a romantic mood and makes silver and crystal glitter.

In the Middle Ages in Europe, tallow candles (*chandelles*) came into use. Made of animal fat, these candles emitted a terrible odor. Handheld candleholders were created for practical purposes. In fact, the French word *chandelier* means a holder for tallow candles. During the eighteenth century, the more expensive and pleasant-smelling beeswax candles (*bougies*) became popular among the wealthy. Since they had to be snuffed out, these candles were normally set at a convenient height on the table or on the mantel.

In a typical eighteenth-century upper-class household, different types of candlesticks were used in different settings. Wooden ones were usually found in the kitchen and other working quarters. In reception rooms (*salons*) silver candlesticks (or *bougeoirs*, which means having a *bougie*) became fashionable, along with candlesticks with arms (*bras*), called candelabra. Literally meaning "tree of candles," candelabras were often made of ormolu (powdered gold). The French *flambeau* (a candlestick with a single holder) was also a favorite due to its simplicity and elegance. On the other end of the spectrum, grand table displays included a girandole—either a candelabra with cut-glass pendants or with a stem composed of figurines, which was showy and magnificent.

Candlesticks come in all sorts of materials, including glass, porcelain, metal, or silver; heights; shapes; and colors. The ideal candlestick is between 7 or 11 inches tall, which allows the candle above to cast a wide light. My favorites candles are colored, in shades of green, orange, or purple, and 7 inches tall. I like simple candlesticks arranged on a table in groupings of three—uneven numbers make for a dynamic composition. I also like to mix different heights, shapes, and colors. It all depends on the mood I want to convey with my table setting. One important consideration is that the candlesticks set on a table should not block your guests' view across the table. And, never place scented candles near food or on the dining table.

To make candles burn slower, wrap them in aluminum foil and put them in the refrigerator for 2 hours before lighting them.

Purchase drip-free candles as they will not harm your tablecloth.

CANDLESTICK AND CANDELABRA CARE

Take extra care when washing a candlestick with a felt-covered base. Do not immerse it in water. Instead, wash it upside down or wipe it with a damp cloth. To remove wax drippings from an intricate candelabra, turn it upside down and hold it over a piece of newspaper. Blow hot air from a hair dryer to melt the wax. To remove wax drippings from silver candlesticks, put them in the freezer. After the wax freezes, it will peel off easily.

Centerpieces and Other Tabletop Accents

In eighteenth-century France, grand tables had a *surtout de table*—a decorative mirrored or silvered platform—in the center of the table. This platform, made from a single piece of silver or gold, was covered with an assemblage of special things, such as exotic spices, oil and vinegar in cruets, candleholders, and candelabras.

The main rule of thumb for centerpieces is to keep them low and unobtrusive. It's not good form to create tall centerpieces as they obstruct your guests' views across the table and make conversations difficult. For formal settings, make sure that the centerpiece is positioned perfectly in the middle of the table. My choice centerpiece is either a silver tray or a mirror with a small vase of flowers placed in the middle. I surround the tray or mirror with candlesticks, small crystal cups full of candy, and salt and pepper holders. For more casual settings, consider a long-stem rose or a beautiful lily in an elegant vase.

Certain small accessories can add interest to a tabletop. Place-card holders are a favorite of mine. They come in a variety of materials—from porcelain to silver—and in interesting shapes, such as miniature chairs, squirrels, dogs, and even deer heads. A diminutive knife rest is also a charming note. Made in materials such as earthenware, porcelain, silver plate, and cut crystal, knife rests, which are generally rectangular, can also have exotic shapes—like fanciful fish, dogs, and even birds. They bring a whimsical touch to your table. Besides, knife rests are fun to collect.

Tea, Coffee, and Chocolate

I always offer a tea and coffee service after dinner, serving all the accouterments on a large tray that includes cups, saucers, a teapot, a coffeepot, a creamer, a sugar bowl, and of course chocolates. Guests are encouraged to pour their own coffee and tea. I find that everyone loves my tradition. I like to serve green tea and occasionally fresh mint leaves steeped in boiling water, along with a strong coffee.

During the seventeenth century, Dutch traders introduced tea to Europe. The French discovered it around 1636, and Louis XIV quickly became a fervent consumer after receiving a solid gold teacup from the King of Siam.

In eighteenth-century France, tea was often served on a buffet (sideboard) during grand balls. All sorts of implements were required to make a tea tray complete. I love teapots—the more unusual the better. I have assembled a wonderful collection. Note that coffeepots are more available on the market than teapots and therefore less expensive. To my mind, a teapot is essential for brewing a good cup of tea. Using loose tea leaves placed in perforated sterling or silver-plated tea balls is ideal. Tea balls are generally round, oval, or egg shaped, and they are often engraved or embossed. Besides serving a necessary function, delicate tea strainers look lovely on a tea tray. A tea cozy is a quilted cover that keeps tea warm in its pot for hours at a time—no small accomplishment. It can be made of lace, needlepoint, patchwork fabric, or even straw. I love them and am always on the lookout for pretty ones that will fit over my teapots and coffeepots.

Coffee was cultivated in Abyssinia and arrived in Europe around 1630. About 1850 it was imported on a large scale to France and

soon became the preferred drink of the aristocracy. Eventually it overtook tea in popularity and became a staple of the cafes named in its honor.

The invention of a cup with a handle is attributed to the Meissen porcelain factory in the first half of the eighteenth century. The delicacy of soft-paste porcelain made it an ideal material for teacups and coffee cups, which were painted by the period's best masters.

Collect teacups and coffee cups from tag sales and flea markets. Just keep in mind the finer the cup's material, the better it is. Be on the lookout for bone china teacups. Create a mismatched set, but stick to the same theme—white and gold, for example, or a similar colorful design, but make sure the saucers match for a more polished look. If you find a set of cups without matching saucers, do not assume that they all have been broken. In the eighteenth century many people preferred pairing sterling-silver saucers with their cups. I like to use my grandmother's Sarreguemines set mixed in with other pieces that I've accumulated over the years.

According to legend, the cocoa tree was the most beautiful in the Aztec paradise. Many virtues were attributed to it, including chocolate-making. In 1615 Anne of Austria, who had married Louis XIII, introduced chocolate to the French court. It was not until the time of the Régence, under Louis XV, that chocolate became fashionable. A special pot, a tall vessel often shaped like a truncated cone with a spout and a horizontal wooden handle, was even created for serving hot chocolate. Similar in shape to a coffeepot, it was usually made of either solid or plated silver, porcelain, or earthenware. At the time connoisseurs advised that good chocolate had to be made the day before in an earthenware pot and left overnight. Such a practice did not endure, but hot chocolate remains a favorite treat for adults and children alike. And eating chocolates with tea or coffee is always enjoyable. Chocolate-dipped lemon peels or candied ginger are my favorites.

TEAPOTS, COFFEEPOTS, CHOCOLATE POTS, AND CUPS CARE

Be gentle when cleaning these fragile pieces.

❦

For stains inside teapots and cups, fill the pieces with a solution of about 1 or 2 teaspoons baking soda and water. Leave until the stains disappear, and then rinse.

For stubborn stains, use a solution of about 1 or 2 teaspoons baking soda and ¼ cup white distilled vinegar.

For tea-stain buildup in teacups, rub a little bit of egg yolk on the stain. Then rub some freshly squeezed lemon juice onto the stain. Clean with a soapy sponge and rinse in water.

Polish the wooden handle of a silver teapot or coffeepot with beeswax before cleaning the silver parts. This will protect the wooden handle from water damage when you clean the silver parts.

❦

CASUAL ENTERTAINING OUTDOORS

Picnics

Nothing is more fun on a warm, sunny day than a picnic with family and friends. And so what if a little bit of dirt finds its way into your picnic fare? Or, if a colony of ants falls in love with your dessert and establishes a camp on the blanket? You will survive. This is part of the pleasure and a celebration of nature.

A picnic is a simple way to start to entertain, especially for an inexperienced host or hostess. Very few rules need to be followed. Start with a large basket and fill it with a colorful cotton tablecloth, plates (paper, plastic, or my favorite, tin), glasses (they come in all sorts of shapes and designs and can be easily purchased through mail-order catalogues), cutlery (useful even though most of the fare will be finger food), napkins, and drinks in bottles placed in a cooler. Don't forget a bottle opener. Salt and pepper shakers are also essential for a civilized party. And then there is the food. Delicious sandwiches on crusty French bread, accompanied by a selection of cheeses and fruits, are divine. Fresh melon, skinned and sliced, with prosciutto, is an easy finger food. Bring the makings for a tomato and mozzarella platter (see page 225). Omelette cake, served with ripe tomatoes and fresh basil, is not only tasty but also healthy. Dry saucisson sliced very thin, paté, and radishes are nice to nibble on as you sip wine, fizzy water, or other kinds of drink. Potato chips and mixed vegetables are also favorites. Don't skimp on dessert. Pack fresh fruits, such as peaches, watermelon, and cherries. Lemon pound cake, chocolate cake cut into small squares, madeleines (see page 227 for Chocolate Chip Madeleines recipe), and an assortment of cookies, such as macaroons (see page 227 for Walnut Macaroons recipe), are the perfect ending to a memorable excursion.

Lunch on the Terrace

Another easy and informal way to entertain during the summer is to serve lunch on the terrace. Prepare ahead of time, making sure that you've cooked certain dishes the night before. Make a tasty meatloaf by marinating a mix of several kinds of ground meat (see page 225 for French Meatloaf recipe). Do not let your family dog come too close when the meatloaf is done. Otherwise you may lose your main course. This has happened to me.

Next prepare the vegetables and dessert. Fresh corn at this time of the year is delicious. If there are children around, have them husk the corn. When completed, place the corn in a large cooking pot with water and 2 cups of milk. Milk will have the double benefit of making your corn sweeter and allowing it to cook for as long as you want without being

overcooked. Green salad is also wonderful during the warm weather months (see how to make a green salad on page 75). To remember how to do perfect vinaigrette (see page 70 for Vinaigrette recipe), follow this witty saying: "An avaricious man for the vinegar, a sage for salt and pepper, a spendthrift for oil, and a fool to turn it." To jazz up the vinaigrette, add some new onions, sliced thin, and two hard-boiled eggs, or a small amount of minced garlic. Or, serve Asparagus with Vinaigrette (see page 226 for recipe). A quiche made with ham, cheese, or vegetables is also always a good main course (see page 33 for two easy-to-make quiche recipes). Desserts always receive attention from me. Clafoutis, a French fruit flan with fresh or canned pitted cherries

or other fruits, such as plum or apricots, is delicious and can be made easily and quickly. Rhubarb Pie (see page 80 for recipe) is equally satisfying. For me, my favorite dessert is My Grandmother's Rice Pudding (see page 226 for recipe).

Now turn to the decoration of the table. Make sure to enlist the help of any available children. Have fun. Pick some large leaves from your garden and use them as place mats. Add colorful napkins. They will give a fresh look to your table with a minimum of expense. For a centerpiece, put the strawberries that you will serve with dessert in a pretty bowl, or heap shiny eggplants mixed with pears or apples (or use whatever fresh fruit you happen to have on hand) on the center of the table.

MAKES 6 TO 8 SERVINGS

This hardy meatloaf is wonderful served hot or cold. It is also perfect for picnic fare as the slices make tasty sandwiches. Make it the night before the outing.

2 tablespoons balsamic vinegar

1 tablespoon extra-virgin olive oil

1 drop of hot chili sauce

1 teaspoon finely chopped fresh thyme

Freshly ground black pepper, to taste

½ teaspoon minced garlic cloves, divided

2 pounds mixed ground meats (such as beef, pork, lamb, and veal)

3 large eggs, lightly beaten

1 small onion, finely chopped

2 hard-boiled eggs, peeled (optional)

12 slices bacon

1. To make the marinade: In a medium-size bowl, mix together balsamic vinegar, olive oil, hot chili sauce, thyme, black pepper, and ¼ teaspoon garlic.

2. Knead the ground meats with your hands until well blended. Place the ground meat mixture with the marinade in a large Ziploc bag overnight (even a couple of hours will do) in the refrigerator.

3. When ready to cook the meatloaf, preheat the oven to 350°F.

4. Place the marinated ground meat in a large bowl. Add the eggs, onion, and ¼ teaspoon garlic. Mix well.

5. Shape the meat mixture into a long sausage-shaped roll. If using the hard-boiled eggs, flatten the roll on a large piece of parchment or waxed paper. Arrange the hard-boiled eggs down the middle. Use the paper to help lift up the sides of the meat mixture to cover the eggs. Pinch the meat seam together to keep the eggs in place. Make sure the ends are sealed by pinching them together.

6. Transfer the meatloaf into a glass baking pan, seam-side down if using hard-boiled eggs. Place the bacon slices on top and on the sides.

7. Bake the meatloaf for at least 45 minutes, basting occasionally, until it is firm, cooked through, and lightly browned, and the bacon is crisp. Let rest for 15 minutes, and then cut into 1-inch thick slices and serve.

Fresh-from-the-market fare is always delicious. A platter of tomatoes and mozzarella, dressed up with basil and extra-virgin olive oil, is very simple to prepare.

SERVES 4

Roasting asparagus is an easy way to prepare this versatile vegetable. The addition of my vinaigrette transforms the dish into a satisfying first course. Serve the asparagus on an attractive platter with silver tongs. For a more elegant presentation, sprinkle a little minced parsley or a finely chopped boiled egg on top.

1½ to 2 pounds white or green asparagus, trimmed

2 tablespoons extra-virgin olive oil

Vinaigrette (see page 70 for recipe)

1. Preheat the oven broiler.

2. Place the prepared asparagus on a baking sheet and drizzle with the oil. Roast in the broiler, turning the spears once or twice, until tender but firm, about 10 minutes.

3. Place the roasted spears on a serving platter and pour the vinaigrette on top.

SERVES 6 TO 8

My grandmother made this comforting dessert during the winter. The fragrant smells of vanilla and candied fruit remind me of her.

1 cup raw white rice, rinsed several times in cold water, and well drained

4 large eggs, separated into yolks and whites

¾ cup granulated sugar

½ teaspoon sea salt

½ teaspoon pure vanilla extract

1 quart heavy cream

½ cup seedless golden grapes

¼ cup candied fruits (preferably a mix of cherries, kumquat, and diced lemon)

Good-quality caramel

1. Preheat the oven to 350°F.

2. In a medium saucepan, boil the rice in 3 cups cold water for 5 minutes; reduce the heat and continue cooking until tender, about 25 minutes. Drain off whatever water is left; set aside.

3. In a medium-size bowl, beat the egg yolks. Add the sugar, salt, and vanilla extract. Stir in the heavy cream and cook, stirring constantly, until thickened. Add the cooked rice, raisins, and candied fruits. Whip the egg whites until they stiffen, and gently fold them into the mixture.

4. Spread caramel across the bottom of an 8-inch-round baking dish. Pour the rice mixture on top. Place the baking dish inside a second slightly larger baking dish filled with about 3 cups of water to create a bain-marie. Cook the rice mixture in the bain-marie for 35 minutes in the oven. Cool the rice pudding to room temperature. Flip the cooled pudding onto an attractive plate, with the caramel on top.

CHOCOLATE CHIP MADELEINES

MAKES ABOUT 24 MADELEINES

The addition of chocolate chips to this traditional madeleine recipe will satisfy the chocoholics in your life.

1¼ sticks unsalted butter, plus more for the madeleine molds
1 cup all-purpose flour
1 cup granulated sugar
4 eggs
1 teaspoon rum
½ cup dark chocolate chips
1 tablespoon confectioners' sugar

1. Preheat the oven to 300°F. (Do not bake in a convection oven.) Coat the madeleine molds with butter, dust lightly with flour; set aside.

2. Add the rum, flour, and mix thoroughly.

3. Melt the butter in a small saucepan or bain-marie (double boiler) on low heat. Add the melted butter to the egg mixture and beat until blended. Set aside for 15 minutes.

4. Pour the mixture into the molds. Add about 4 chocolate chips to each mold. Bake for about 10 minutes, or until golden brown. Remove the molds from the oven. Cool the madeleines on a wire rack, and sprinkle with confectioners' sugar when still warm.

WALNUT MACAROONS

MAKES ABOUT 30 MACAROONS

These flourless cookies are crunchy delights. Assemble them on a tiered silver platter to dress up your dessert table.

1 cup granulated sugar
1 cup ground walnuts
5 egg whites
Pinch of sea salt

1. Preheat the oven to 180°F. Line a large baking sheet with parchment paper, and set aside.

2. In a medium-size bowl, mix the sugar and ground walnuts. In a second medium-size bowl, whisk the egg whites with salt until stiff peaks form. Gently fold the egg whites into the walnut mixture.

3. Spoon small heaps of the mixture onto the prepared baking sheet, spacing the dollops 1 inch apart. Bake for 15 minutes, or until golden brown. Lift the macaroons with a spatula, and transfer them to a wire rack to cool.

When family and friends are around, plan some organized activities, such as games and sports. Depending on your surroundings, the following are fun possibilities:

BILLIARDS

The term "billiard" comes from the French words *boules* or *billes*, the name of the ball originally used for the game. The game began in the fifteenth century, and has had an illustrious history. Louis XIV had an elaborate billiard room at Versailles, which was illuminated with twenty-six chandeliers and sixteen floor candelabras. It is no surprise that the fashion for such a room spread throughout the aristocracy (minus the impressive lighting). Thomas Jefferson was so fond of the game that he concealed a billiard room in the dome of Monticello. Abraham Lincoln championed the game, calling it "health inspiring, scientific, and lending recreation to an otherwise tired mind." With such an endorsement, go ahead and play billiards with your friends.

CATCHING AND MOUNTING BUTTERFLIES AND OTHER INSECTS

Insect collecting has had a long history. During eighteenth-century Europe, it became a popular educational hobby. It is still a popular French pastime. Collecting insects is not only educational but also fun. All you need is a net

Collecting butterflies is an educational activity for children and adults alike.

to catch the butterflies, as well as a glass jar, mounting cases, and pins.

CROQUET

Croquet can be traced back to the fourteenth century in France, when it was called paille-maille. Originally an indoor version of lawn bowling, croquet was played during inclement weather but eventually evolved into the outdoor game that we know today. Croquet was an acceptable game for woman to play outdoors in the company of men, although these games of croquet were carefully chaperoned.

Tight croquet, which involved kicking the ball, permitted a young man to go into the bushes with a young woman to look for the ball. Croquet's popularity grew in the 1860s. At that time, garden parties were even called "croquet parties."

HUNTING

During the Stone Age, humans hunted for survival. Today, hunting is considered a sport. It is an opportunity to show off your good aim. Taxidermy trophies of birds and mammals add to the decoration of a room.

PÉTANQUE

Pétanque belongs to a family of ball games that developed in the Mediterranean, known today as *boules* in French and *bocce* in Italian. Around 1907 Jules LeNoir altered an older game known as *jeu Provençal* inventing what eventually evolved into the modern sport of *pétanque*.

PING-PONG

Nothing is more fun than a great game of Ping-Pong, especially after lunch or dinner. It is one of my favorite pastimes. This game got its start in England in the late nineteenth century when, after dinner, some upper-middle-class Victorians turned their dining room table into a miniature version of a traditional lawn tennis court. Several different objects were originally employed: A line of books was used as the net. Rackets were lids from empty cigar boxes, and later, parchment paper was stretched around a frame. The ball was either a ball of string, a champagne cork, or made of rubber. Today, professional tables and equipment are readily available.

ROWING

Rowing goes back to Egyptian times. At the end of seventeenth century in France, it became a fashionable way to pass the time (*passe temps*). During the summer at Versailles under Louis XIV a fleet of gondolas, rowboats, and sailboats sailed in the château's grand canal. Today it is delightful to sit on the grass near the canal and watch people still enjoying this sport.

INDEX

ACKNOWLEDGMENTS

French Chic Living is a tribute to my family and to my French roots.

I wish to extend my heartfelt thanks to my dear friends Michelle and Jean Francis Charrey, who welcomed me into their home and made the photographic part of my book a real pleasure. Without their generosity, *French Chic Living* would not have been possible.

The soulful photographs are the work of Tim Street-Porter. Tim has the rare ability to infuse his beautiful images with charm. We enjoyed our lunches and dinners together, which included some of the edible photography props as well as the planning of shoots at the house, in the garden, or at the farmers' market. And, thank you to Liz Nightingale of Christofle, New York, for generously loaning some of the silver pieces that are featured in the photographs.

A special thank-you to those who helped and advised me during the writing of the manuscript: Martine Longhi, Beatrix Krug, Renate McKnight, Janet Lowry, Nancy Evans, Mary Byrne, Sandra and Hugh Lawson, Terry Campion, David Graff, Jason Rubinstein, Christine McCarty, Dana Schulman, Matthew Patrick Smyth, Jean Vallier, Martine Poivre, Robin Glantz, my sister Catherine Burgio, and Angeline Goreau, along with Annie Kelly and Nabil Nahas, who can always be counted upon for guidance.

Many thanks to my delightful editor Sandy Gilbert for her hard work. She is a terrific, thoughtful editor, full of enthusiasm, and totally dedicated to her projects. And thank you to the lovely Hilary Ney, who is a skilled researcher and writer. Thank you to the rest of the book team: copyeditor Susan Homer, proofreader Elizabeth Smith, and indexer Marilyn Flaig for helping to put the finishing touches on the written words. And, a huge thanks to Jan Derevjanik for her warm and inspiring graphic design— a beautiful presentation of my ideas and the visual images.

It has been a pleasure writing yet another Rizzoli book. My deepest gratitude goes to publisher Charles Miers for his constant support. I am also grateful to Jessica Napp and Ron Longe for their unrelenting publicity efforts, and to the rest of my Rizzoli family.

Finally, thank you to my husband, Sean, for his support, and my children Aymar, Cameron, and Valentina, who are always delighted to see my new book project come to fruition.

Merci.

First published in the
United States of America in 2015
by Rizzoli International Publications, Inc.
300 Park Avenue South
New York, New York 10010

www.rizzoliusa.com

2015 2016 2017 2018 / 10 9 8 7 6 5 4 3 2 1

Printed in China

ISBN 13: 978-0-8478-4637-5

Library of Congress Cataloging-in-Publication
Data: 2015938570

Project Editor: Sandra Gilbert
Design: Jan Derevjanik
Book Production Manager: Kaija Markoe

CREDITS

Thank you to Christofle (us.christofle.com),
experts in the art of table setting since 1830, for
generously loaning silver and silver-plated and
glass items for the photography included in *French
Chic Living* on the following pages:

112 Silver cleaning products and Jardin d'Eden
flatware

113 Malmaison bowl on stand and ice-cream bowl,
Anemone-Belle Époque tray, Albi candlestick, and
Vertigo two-tier pastry stand and two bowls

168 Peuplier silver bud vase

194 Crystal Kawali champagne flutes and goblets,
Vertigo bangle bowl, Anemone-Belle Époque
champagne cooler, Transatlantique centerpiece,
and Malmaison ice spoon

219 Albi candelabra and Malmaison fruit bowl